Dundas Ontario in Colour Photos Book 3, Saving Our History One Photo at a Time

Photography
by Barbara Raué
2012

Series Name:
Cruising Ontario

Book 55: Dundas in Colour Book 3

Cover photo: 1 Victoria Street

Series Name: Cruising Ontario
Saving Our History One Photo at a Time

Photos now in full colour
Check the Appendixes in the back of each book for
descriptions of architectural terms and building styles

Other Books by Barbara Raue

Coins of Gold

Arrows, Indians and Love

The Life and Times of Barbara
Volume 1: Inventions That Have Enhanced My Life
Volume 2: Entertainment That I Have Enjoyed
Volume 3: East Coast Trips
Volume 4: Olympics Have Always Intrigued Me
Volume 5: Wonders of the World
Volume 6: Caribbean Cruises We Have Enjoyed
Volume 7: Animals
Volume 8: Storms and Other Major Disasters in My Lifetime
Volume 9: Wars, Terrorist Attacks and Major Disasters

The Cromwell Family Book

Visit Barbara's website to view all of her books
http://barbararaue.ericraue.com

Dundas, Ontario

Dundas was originally known as Cootes Paradise, named after Captain Cootes of the Kings Royal 8th Regiment and was incorporated as a town in 1847. Its tree lined streets, heritage homes and picturesque downtown reflect the nostalgic quality of the past. Businesses, found in renovated Victorian buildings, were mostly built of limestone or brick after a fire in 1881 destroyed original wooden buildings. Downtown consists of two blocks along King Street West with specialty stores. Fran White, the owner of Heirlooms Bridal Saloon, says the building used to be Hugh Walker's Hardware Store built in 1883. They renovated the building in 1987 but kept the original 14-foot ceilings, wooden floors, long counter and sliding rail ladder. Terraware is a hemp shop where all products are environmentally friendly. Mickey McGuire's Cheese Shop offers a wide selection of cheeses from around the world. Inside the Ukrainian Store there are pirogues, traditional meats and delicious biscuits. The arts helped shape the destiny of Dundas which is home to many artists who have achieved international fame. Off the main street is the Dundas Valley School of Art set in an 1830s one time munitions factory on Ogilvie Street. Learn more Dundas history at the Dundas Museum and Archives on Park Street West. Drive slowly down Victoria Street to admire gorgeous stately historical homes. Taylor's Tearoom is a great place to have lunch or afternoon tea. The Keeping Room is a fabulous kitchen shop.

Index

Melville Street

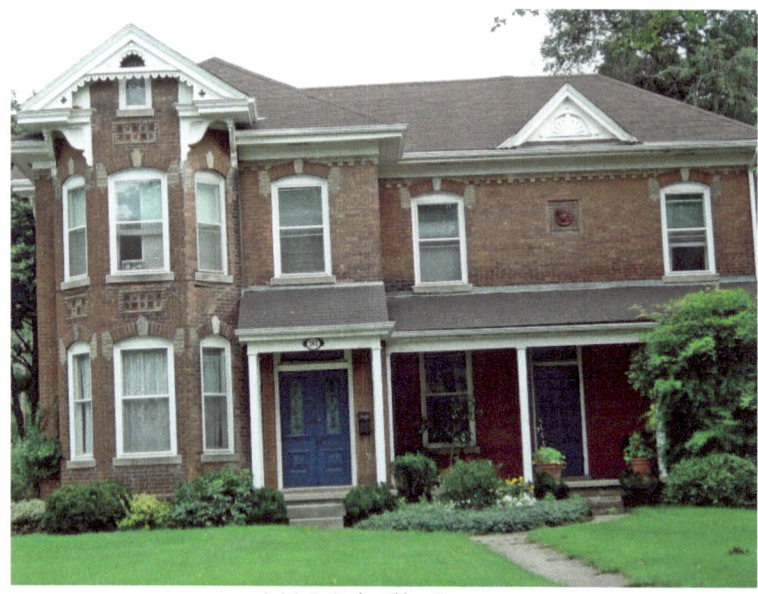

141 Melville Street

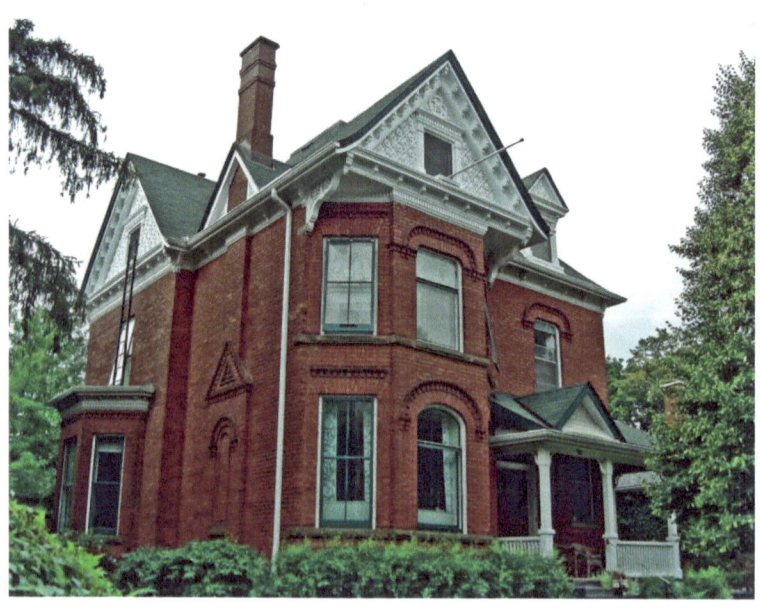

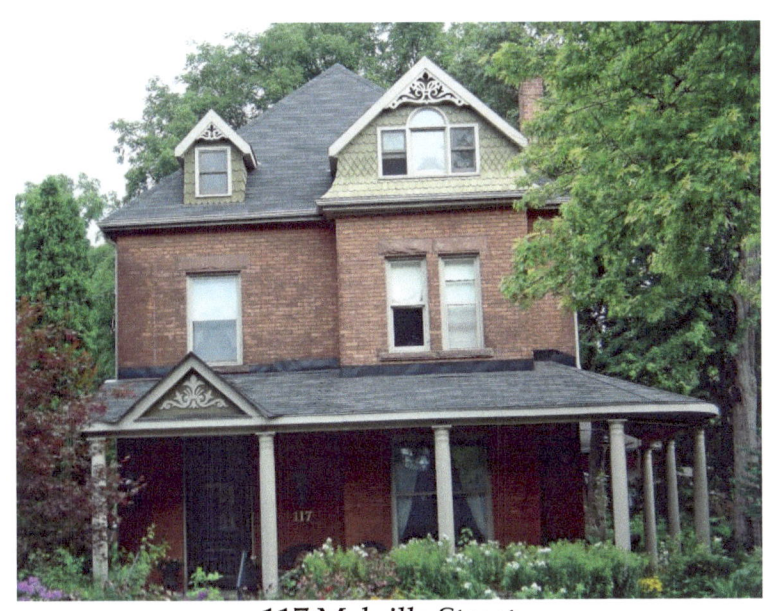

117 Melville Street

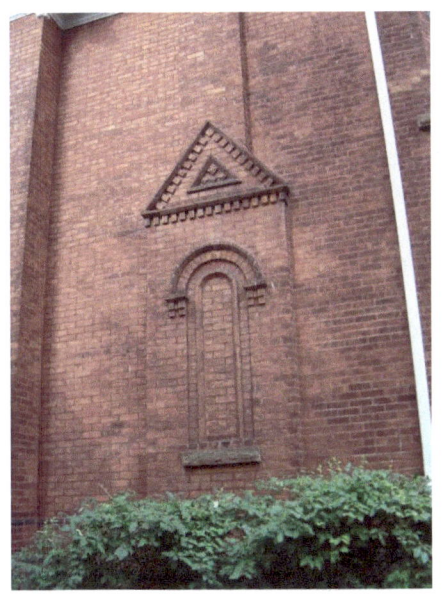

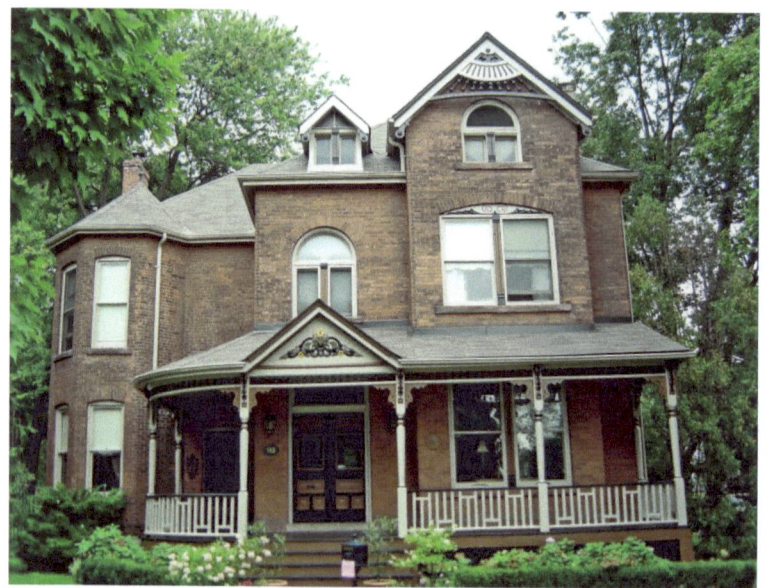

113 Melville Street – Queen Anne style

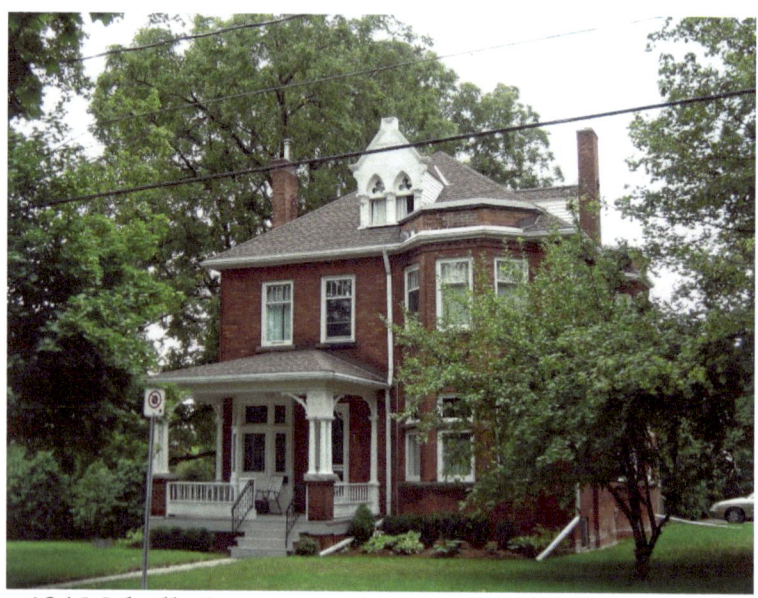

106 Melville Street – Italianate style, dormer in attic

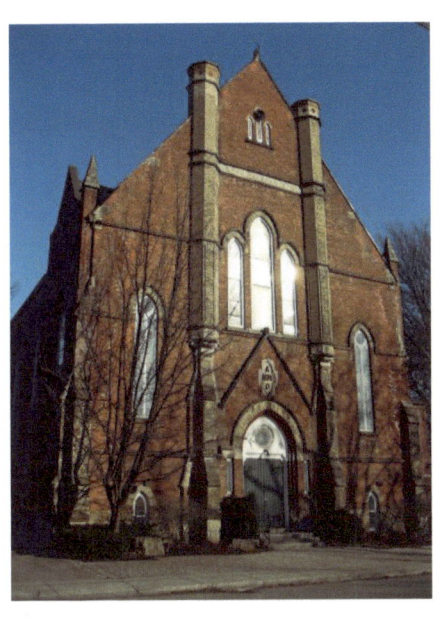

Knox Presbyterian Church – A.D. 1874
Melville Street

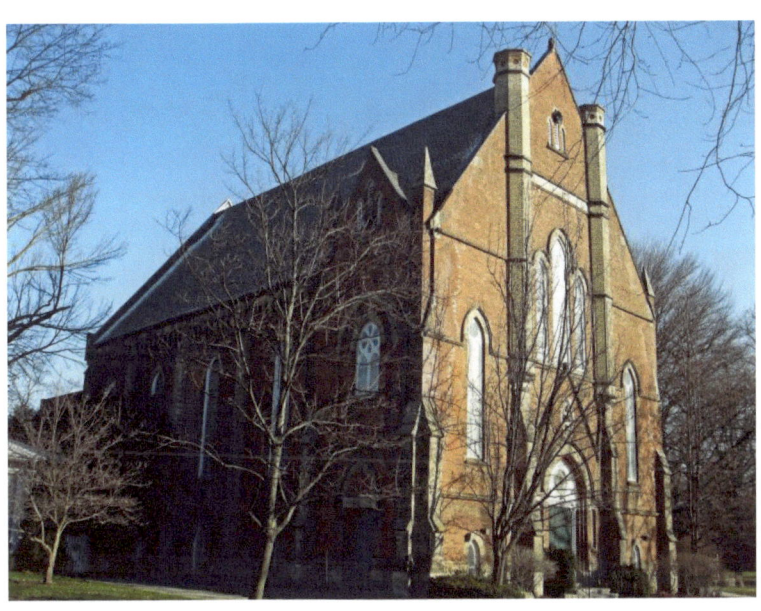

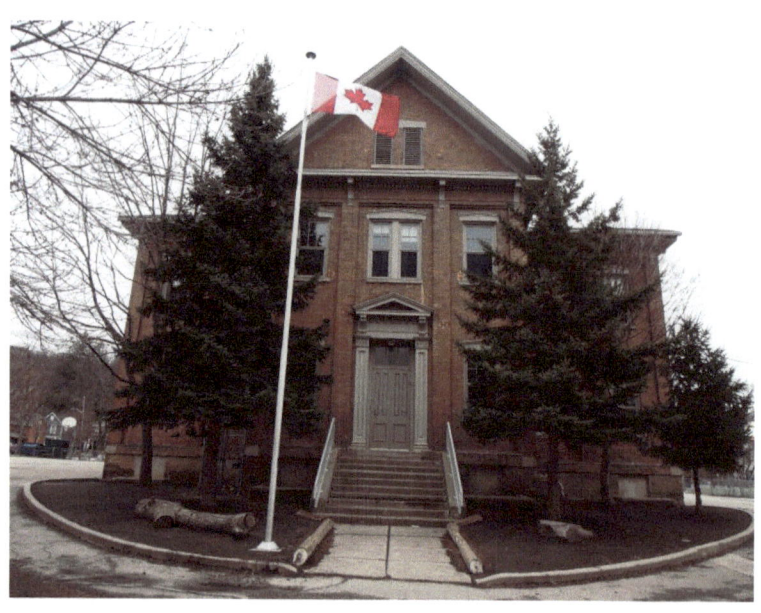

73 Melville Street – Central Public School

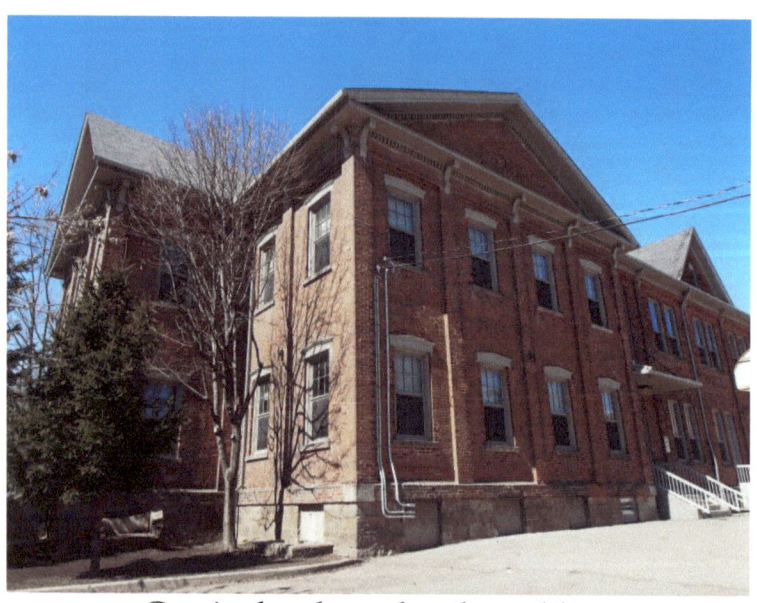

Cornice brackets, dentil moulding

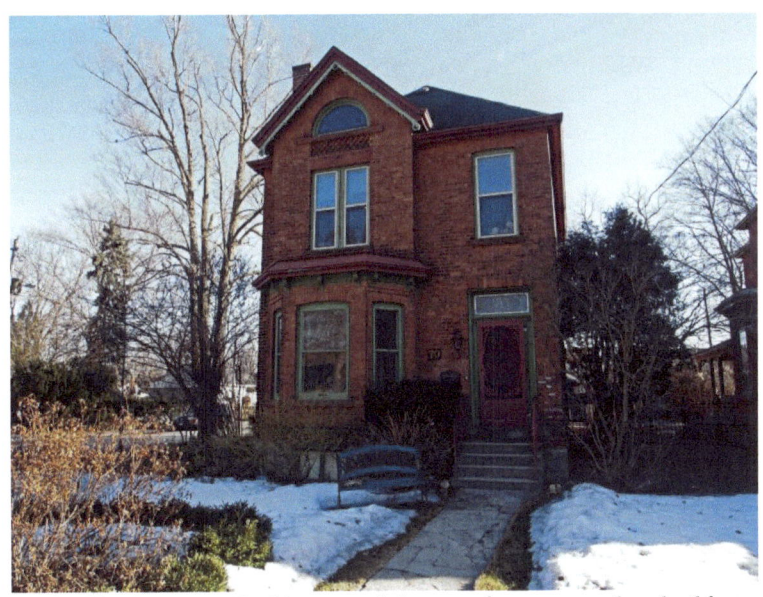

70 Melville Street – Italianate, hip roof, two-and-a-half storey tower-like bay

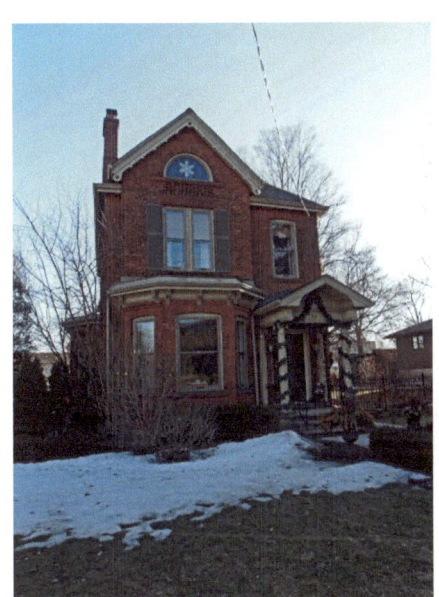

72 Melville Street
Italianate

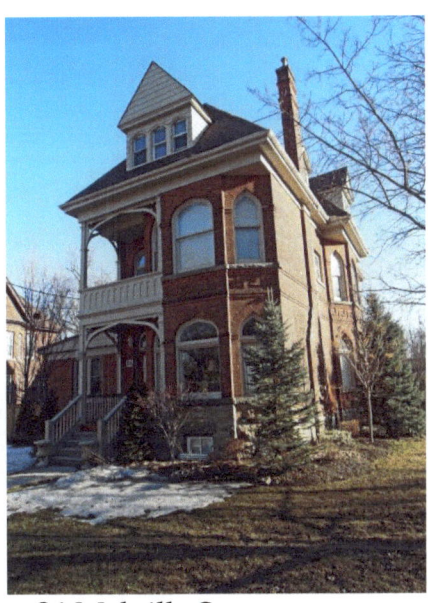

84 Melville Street
Italianate – dormer in attic

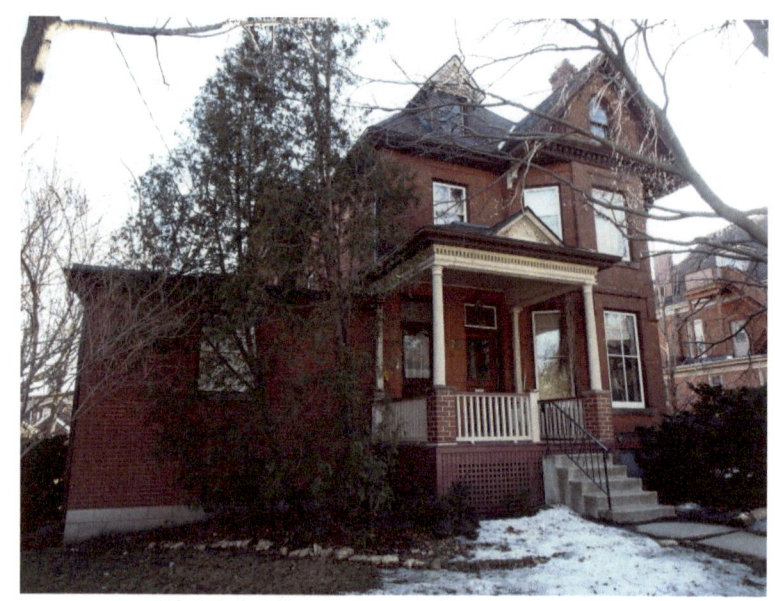

78 Melville Street – dormer in attic

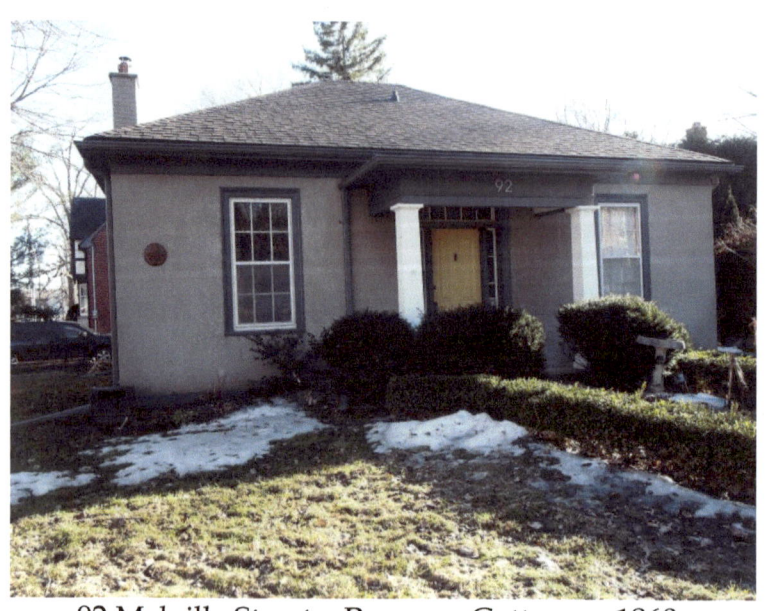

92 Melville Street – Regency Cottage c. 1860s

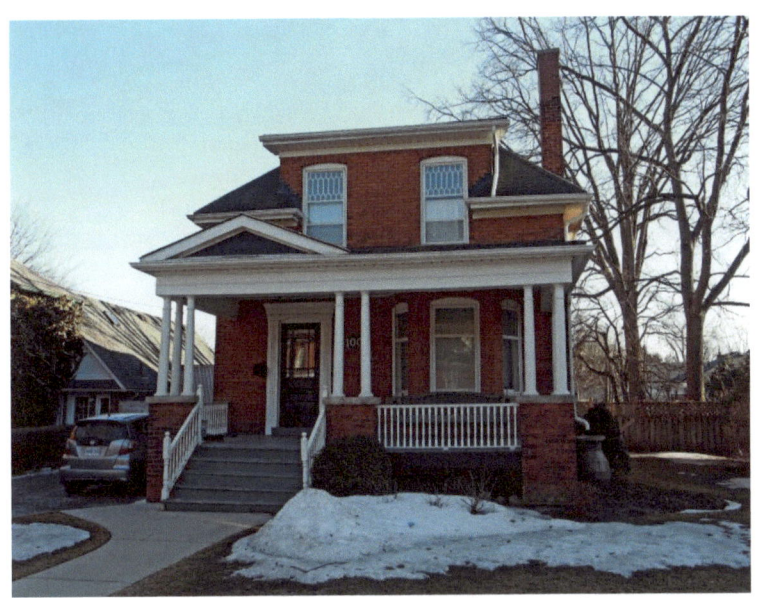

100 Melville Street – Italianate – pediment above entrance

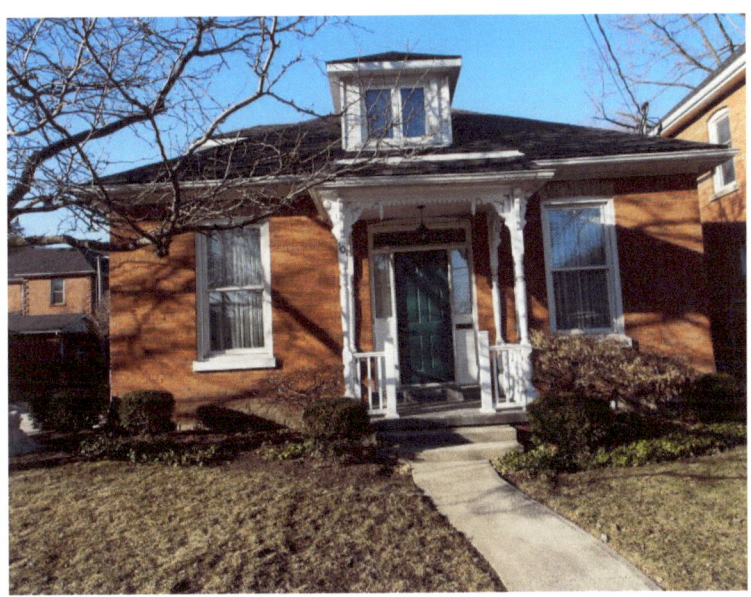

101 Melville Street – Regency Cottage – dormer in attic

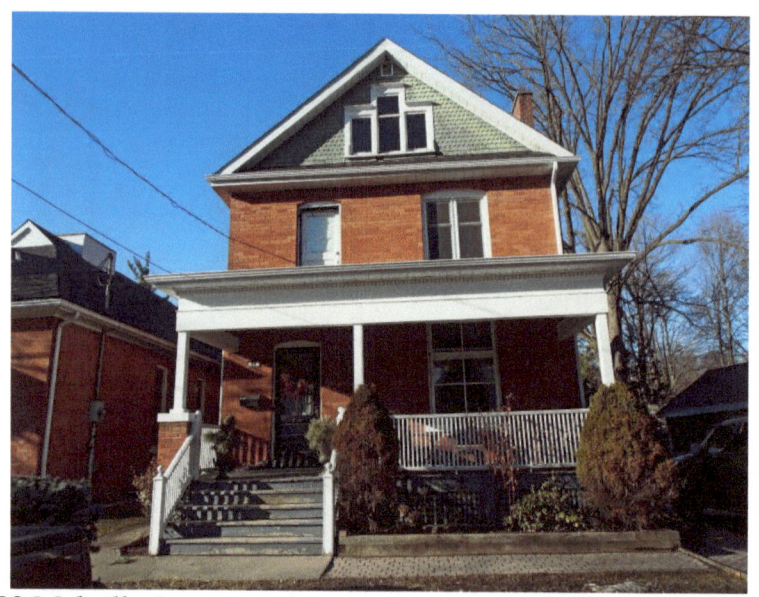

99 Melville Street – Edwardian style – Palladian window

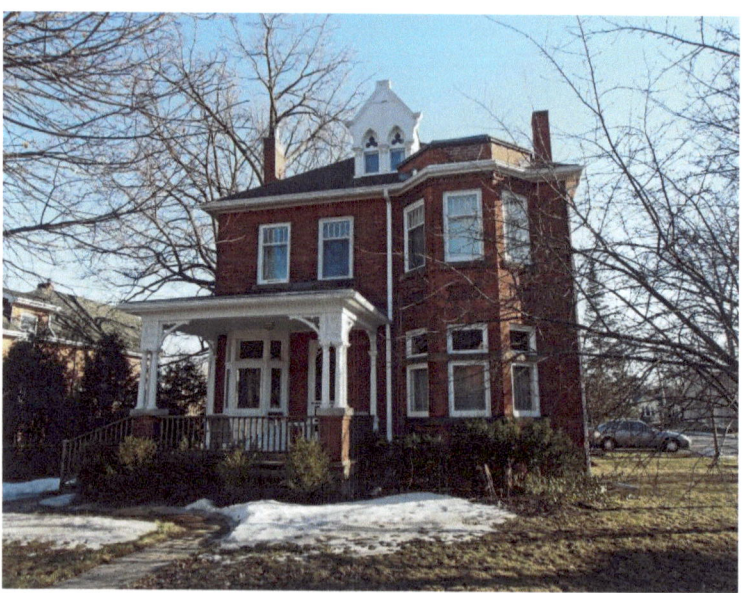

106 Melville Street – Italianate with two-storey tower-like bay, dormer in attic

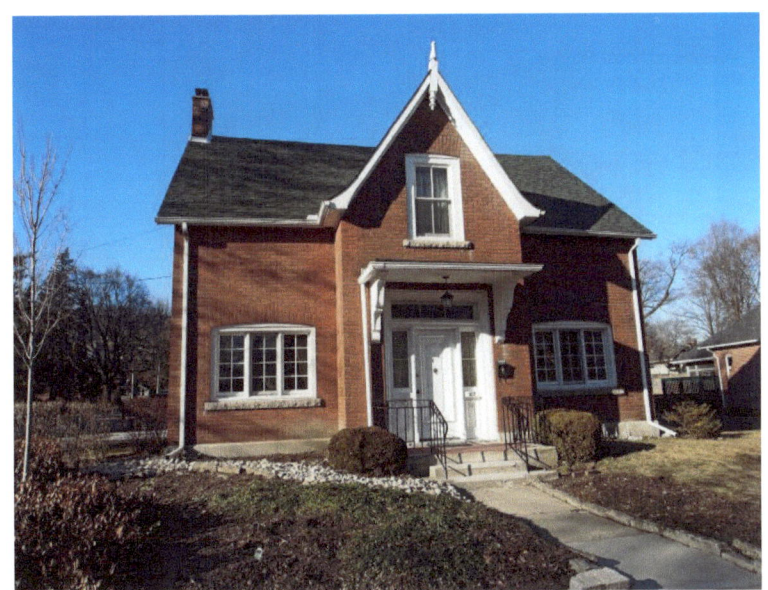

107 Melville Street – Gothic Revival Cottage, finial on gable

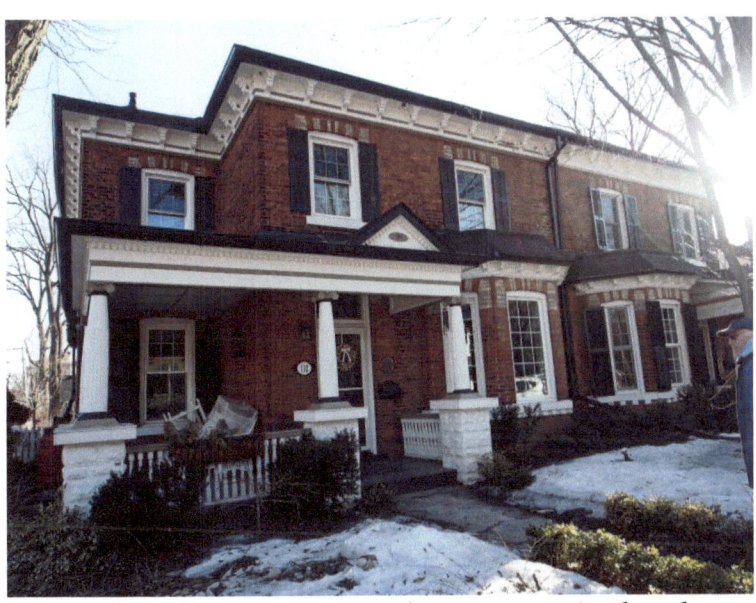

112-114 Melville Street – Italianate, cornice brackets
c. 1880s – pediment above entrance

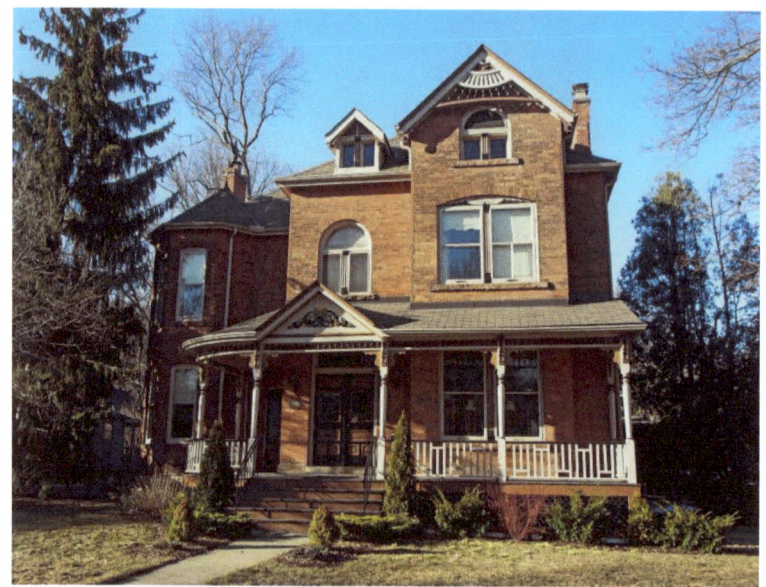

113 Melville Street – Italianate - c. 1890s - two-and-a-half storey tower-like bay, dormer in attic, Vergeboard trim on gable, two-storey bay on side, pediment with decorated tympanum

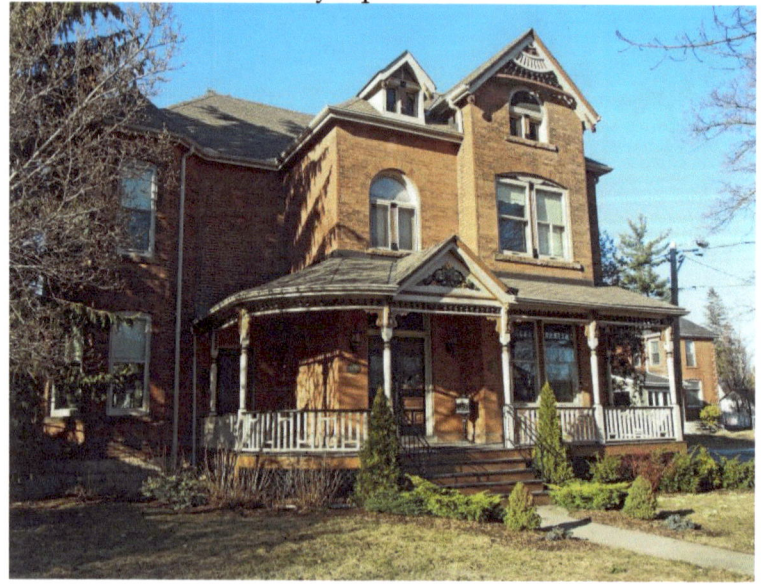

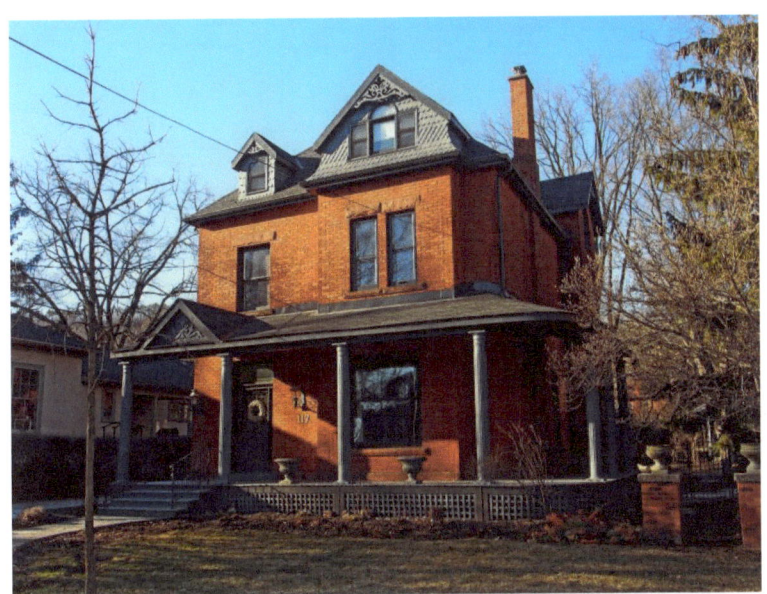

117 Melville Street – Italianate, dormer in attic, Palladian window, Vergeboard trim, decorated tympanum, wrap-around verandah

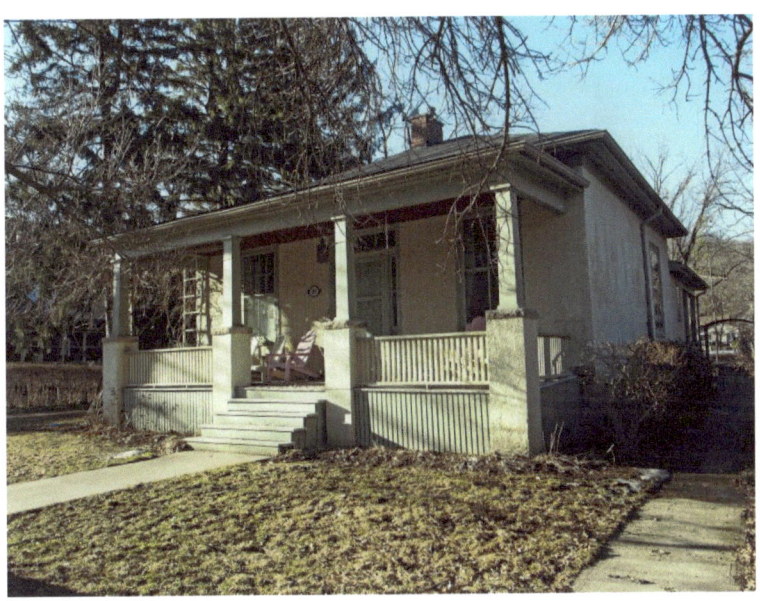

119 Melville Street – one-storey cottage

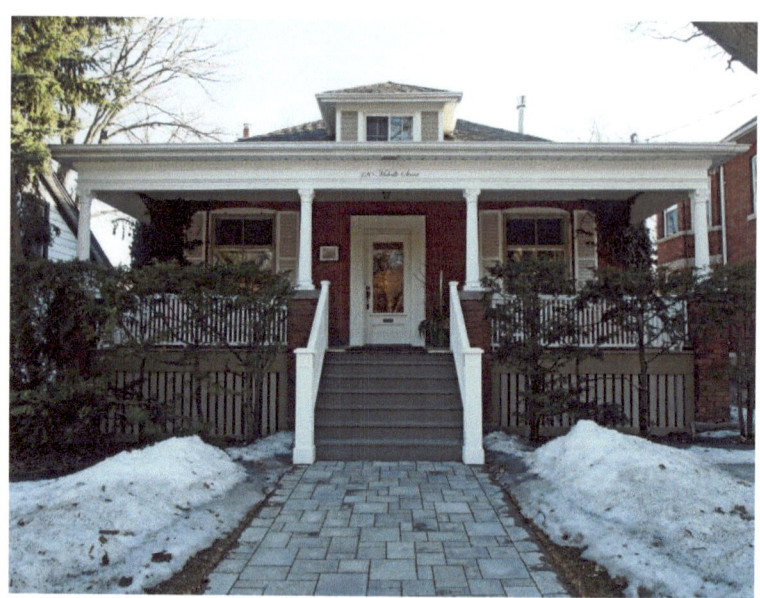

120 Melville Street – Regency Cottage – dormer in attic

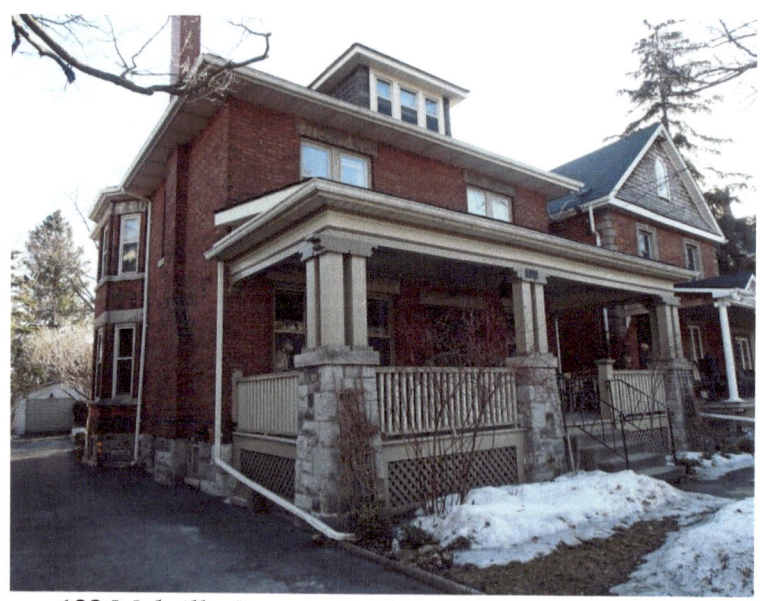

122 Melville Street – Italianate – dormer in attic

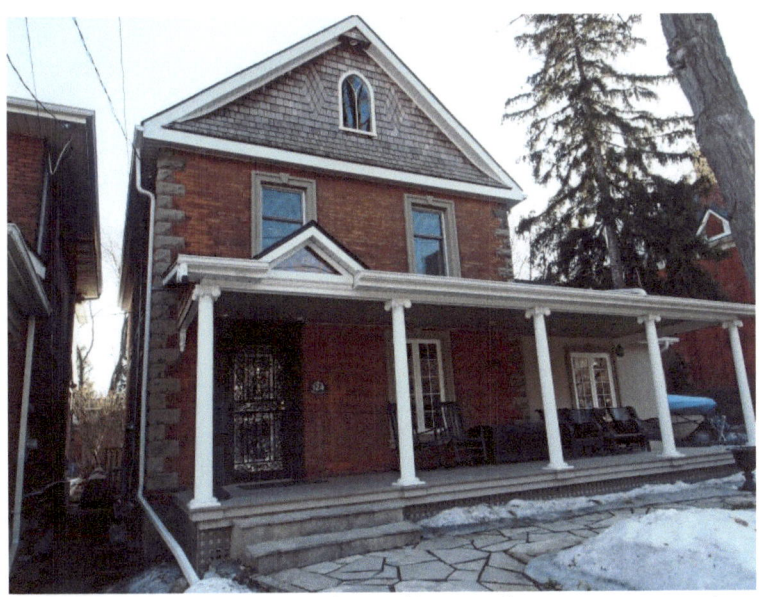

124 Melville Street – Edwardian style – corner quoins

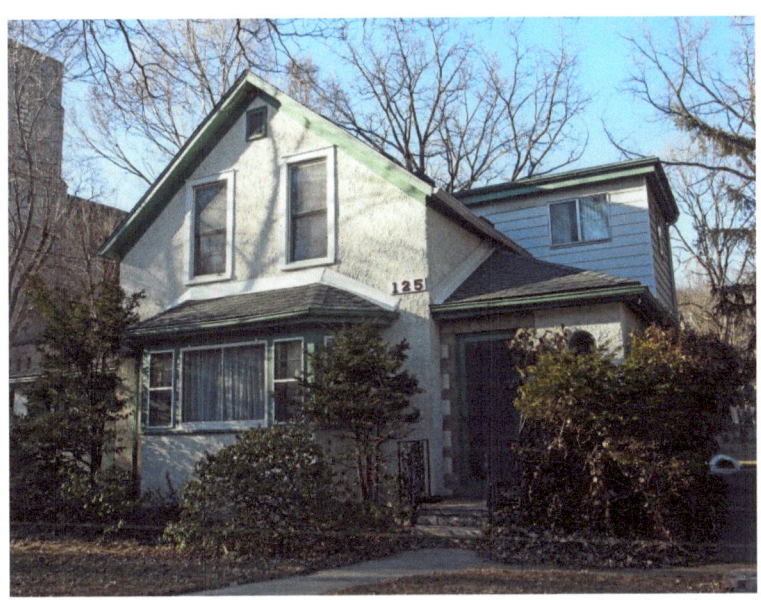

125 Melville Street – Gothic Revival - one-and-a-half storey
stucco

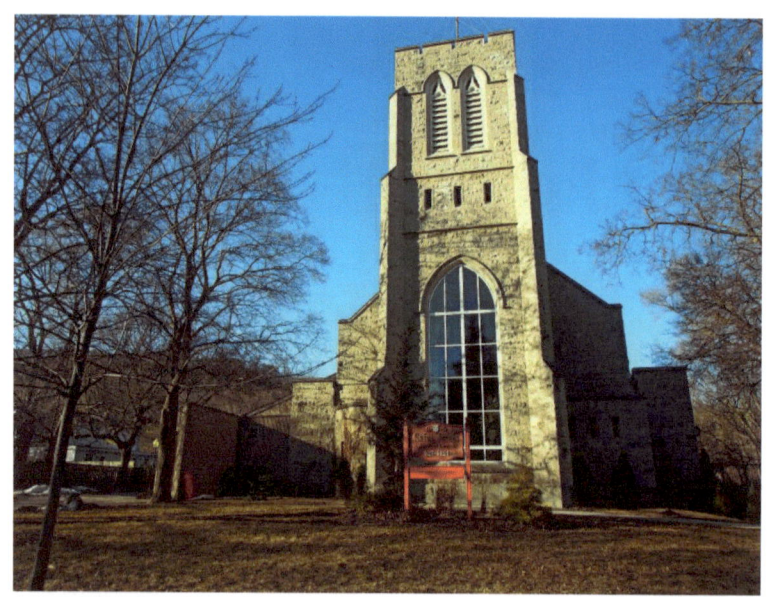

137 Melville Street - St. James Anglican Church

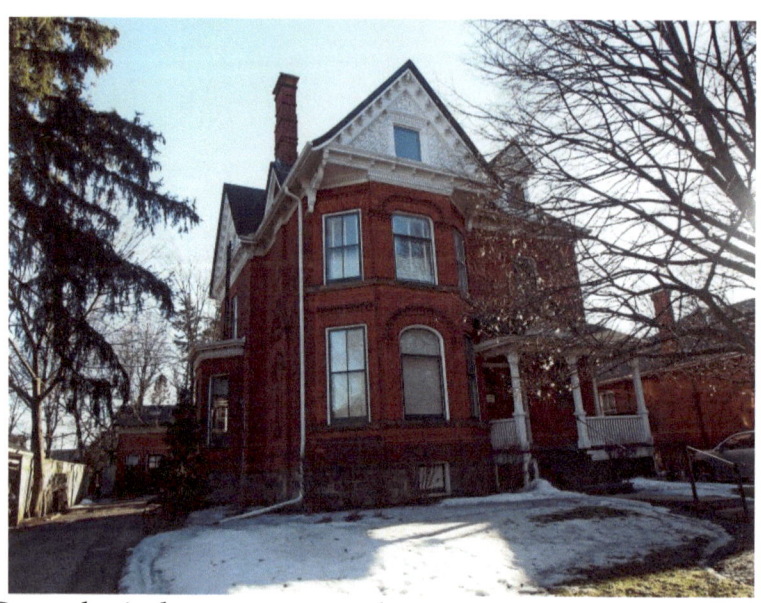

Curved window voussoirs, decorative brickwork, cornice brackets, decorative gable, dormer in attic

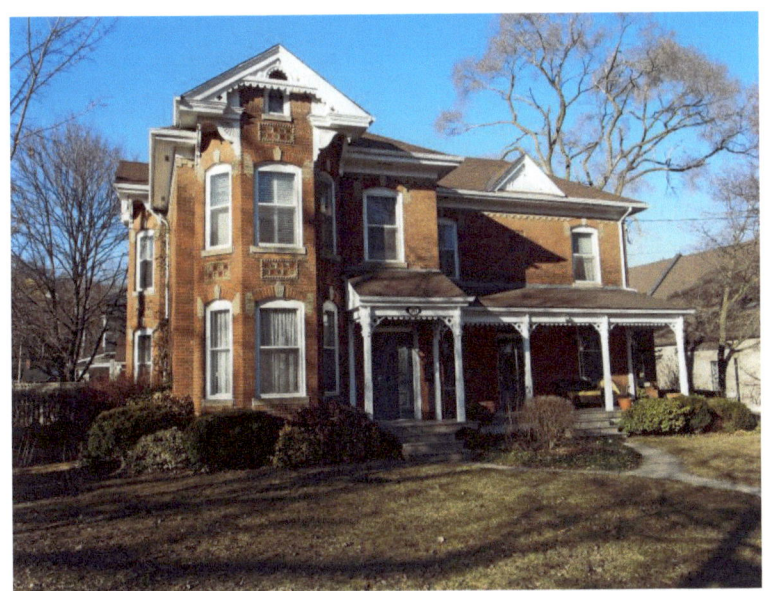

141 Melville Street – Italianate with two-and-a-half storey tower-like bay, vergeboard trim, decorative brickwork, fretwork, dentil moulding, keystones and voussoirs

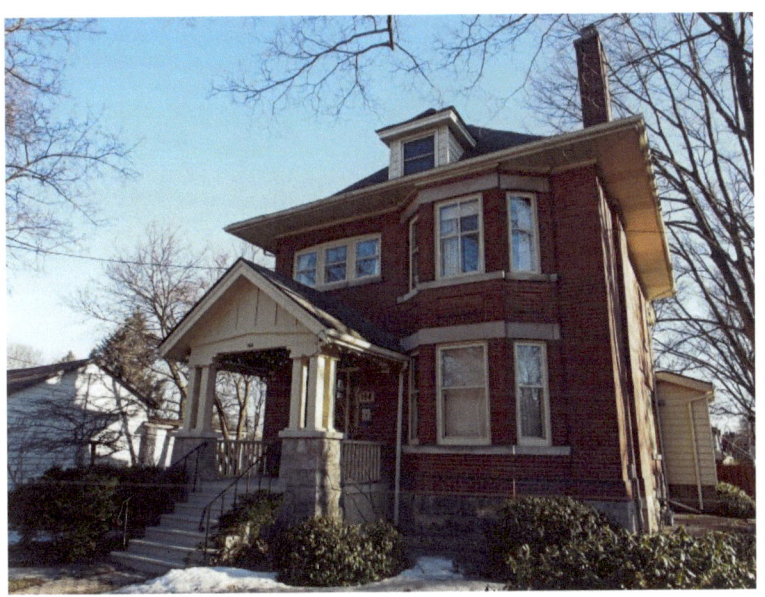

144 Melville Street

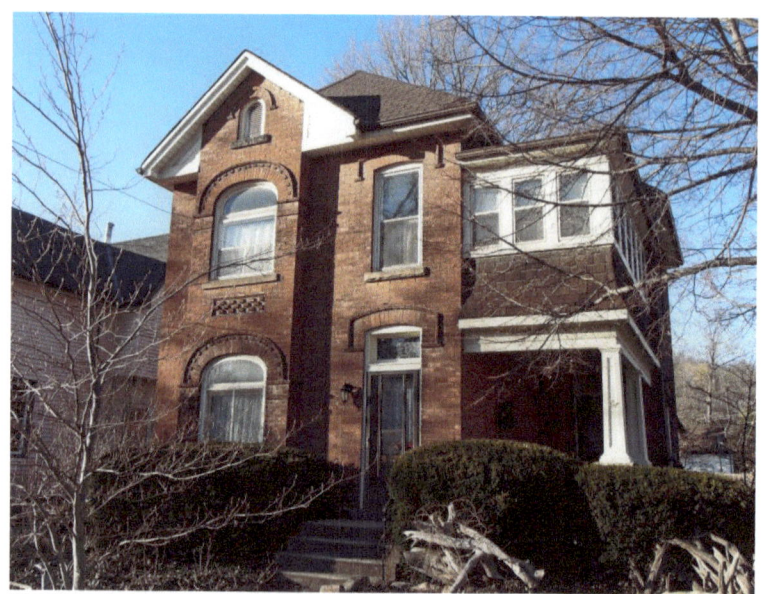

149 Melville Street

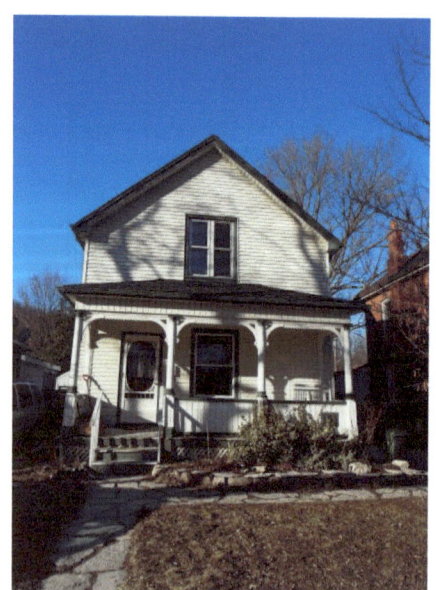

151 Melville Street
Gothic Revival

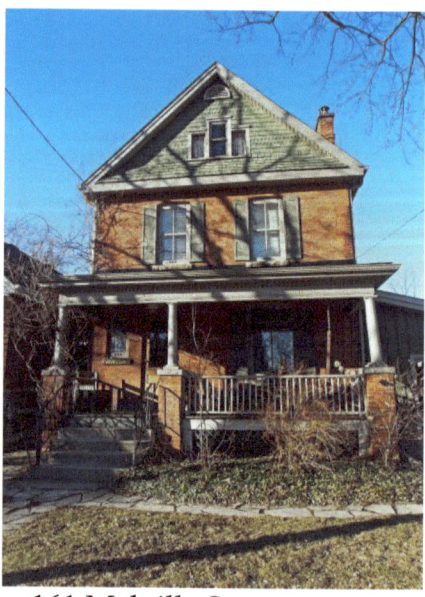

161 Melville Street
Edwardian, Palladian window

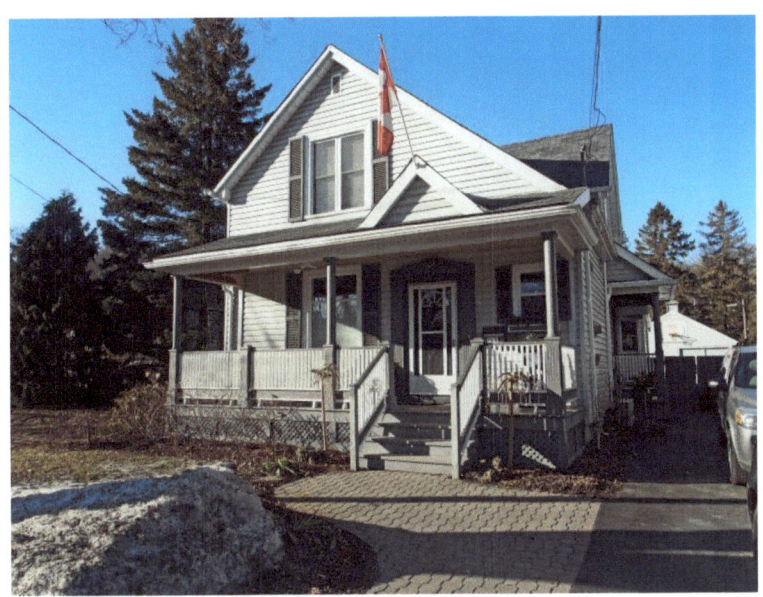

153 Melville Street

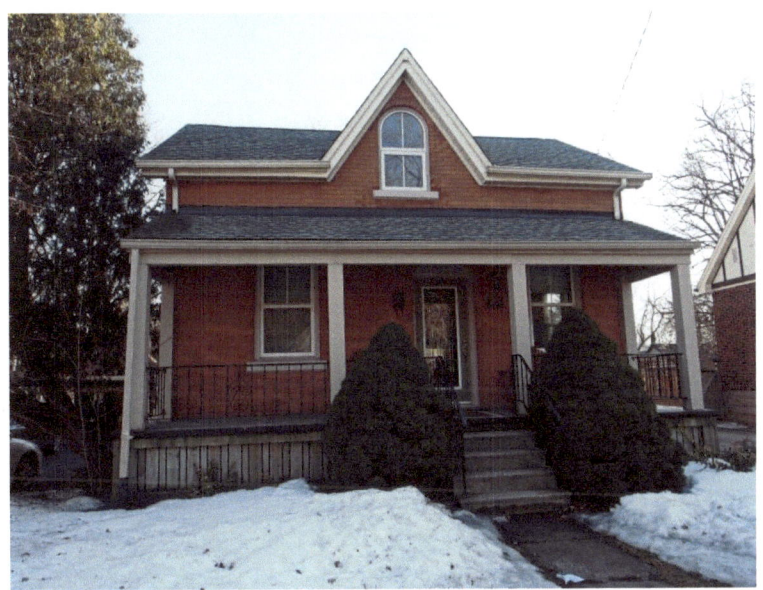

166 Melville Street – Gothic Revival, one-and-a-half storey

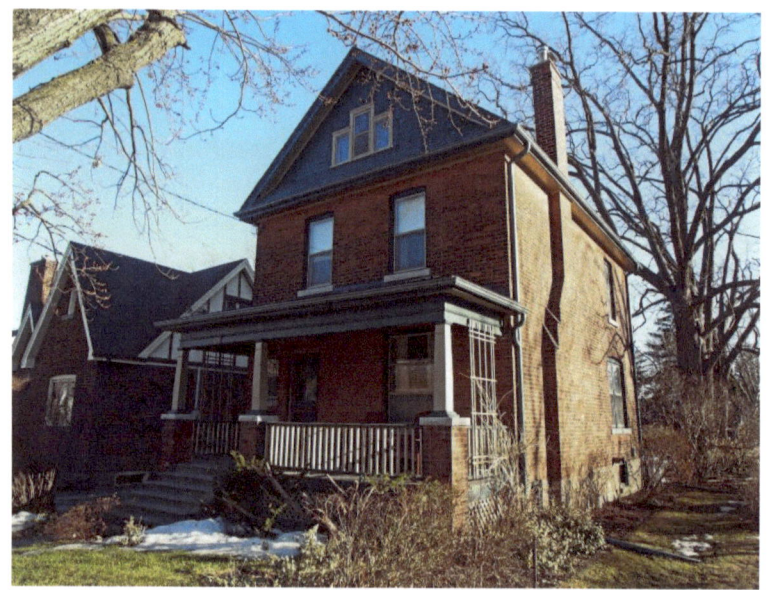

174 Melville Street – Edwardian, Palladian window

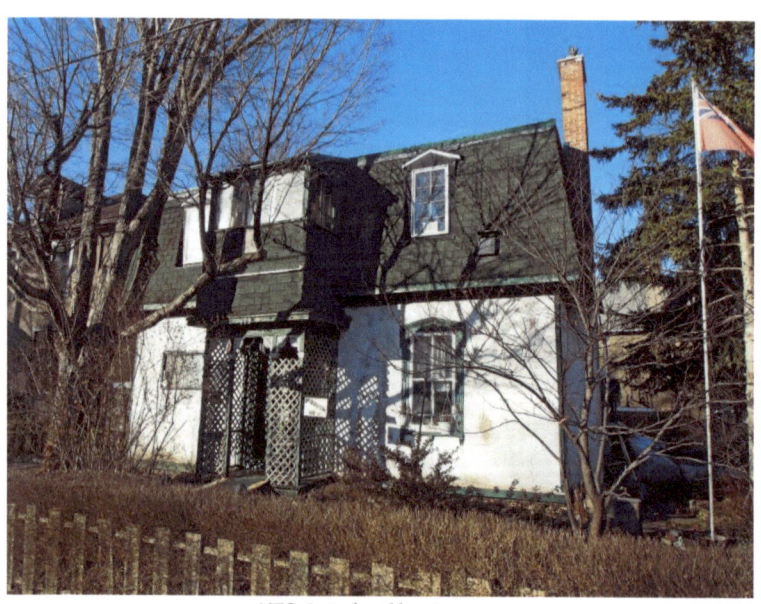

179 Melville Street

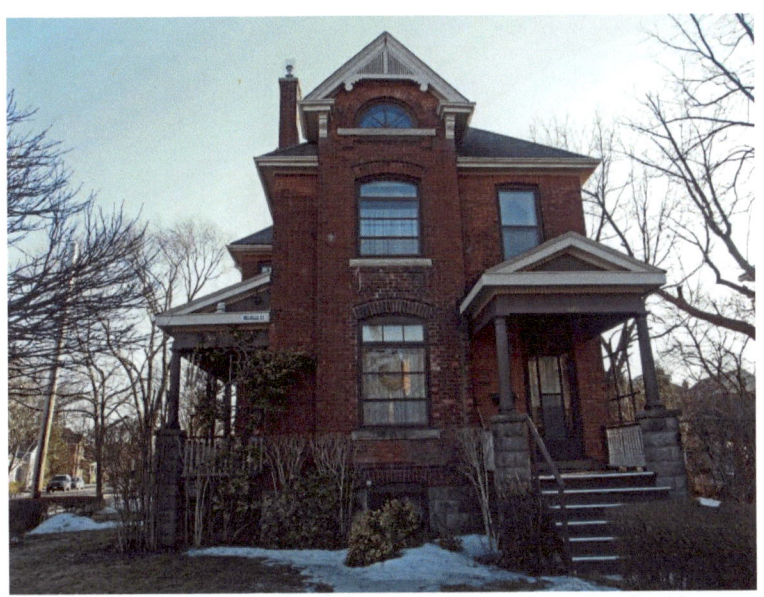

182 Melville Street - Italianate with two-and-a-half storey tower-like bay on front, pediment above verandah, cornice return on gable

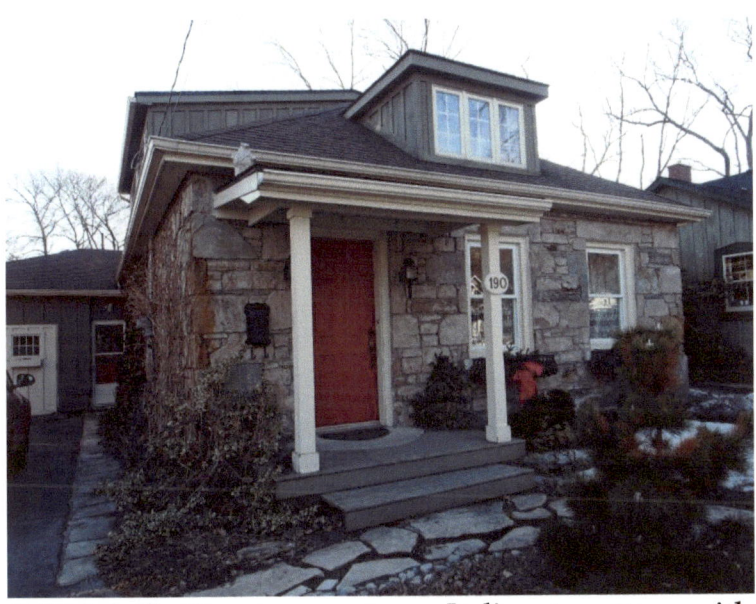

190 Melville Street – one storey Italianate cottage with dormers in attic

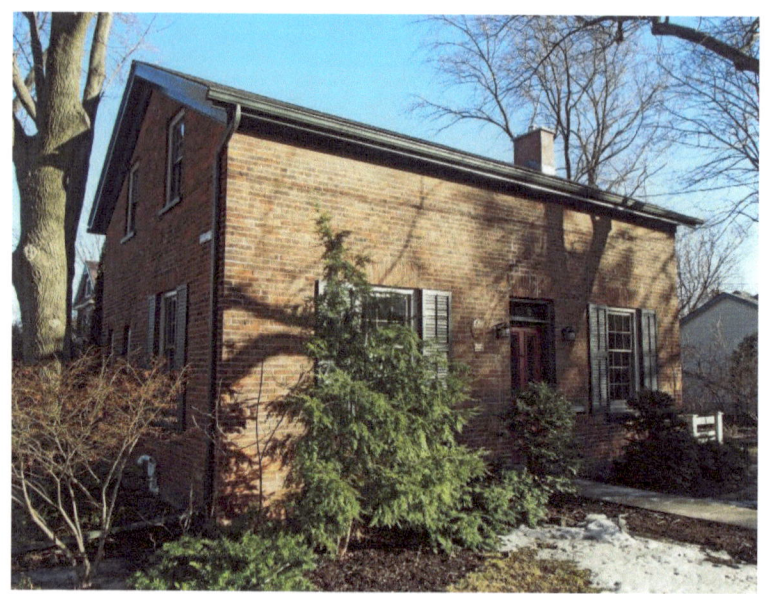

Corner of Melville and Napier Streets – c. 1850s

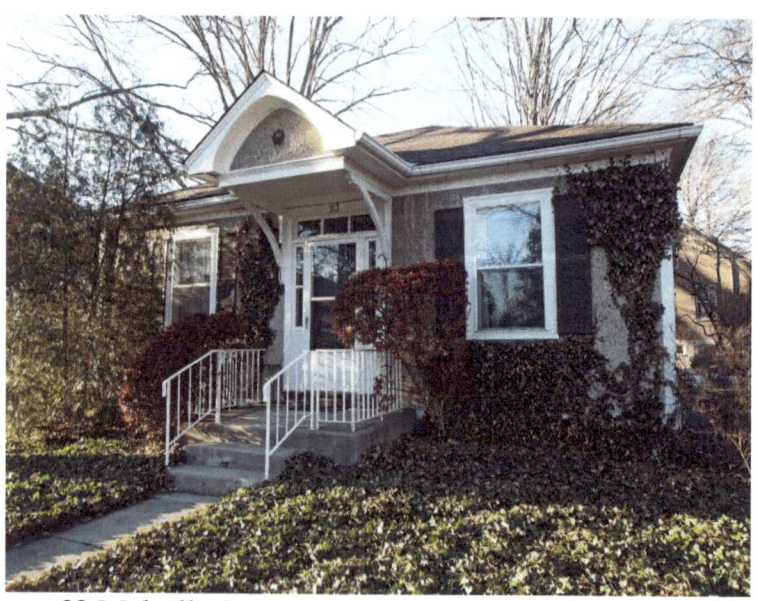

93 Melville Street – Italianate Cottage, hip roof

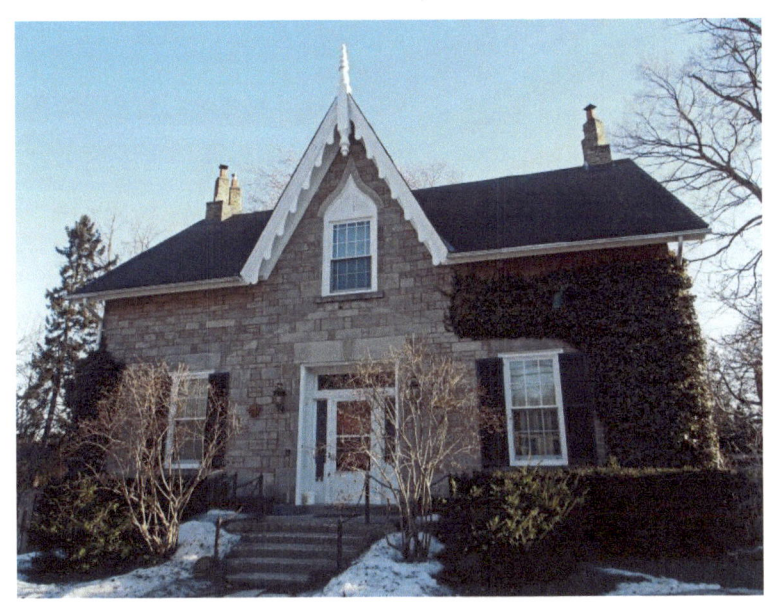

146 Park Street – Gothic Revival – Vergeboard trim on gable
with finial – c. 1850s

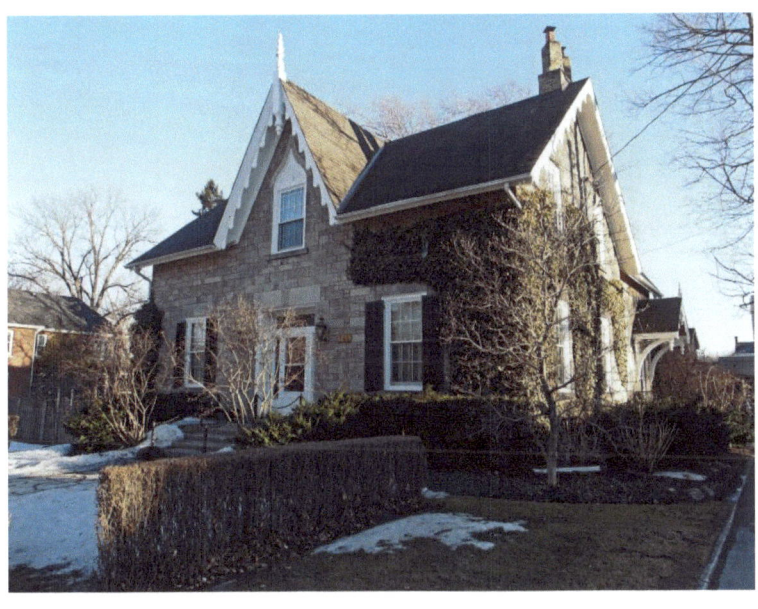

Victoria Street

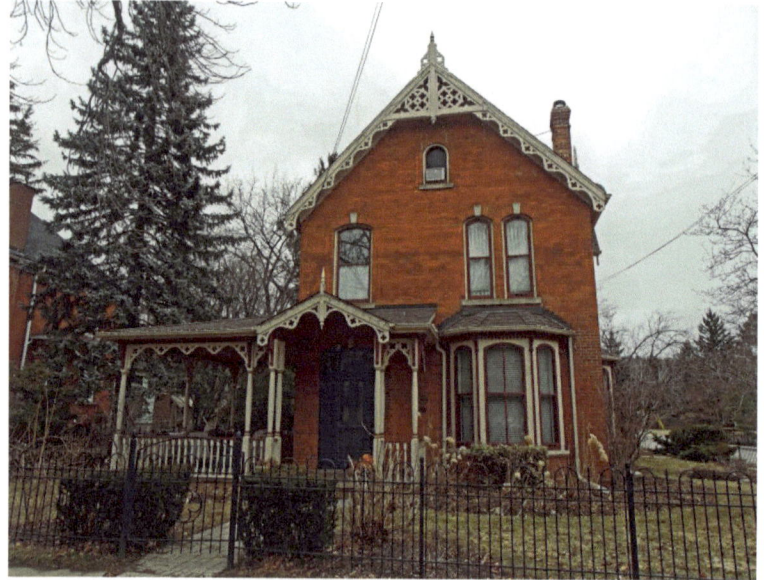

1 Victoria Street - Gothic Revival - circa 1880s – decorative vergeboard, finial on gable

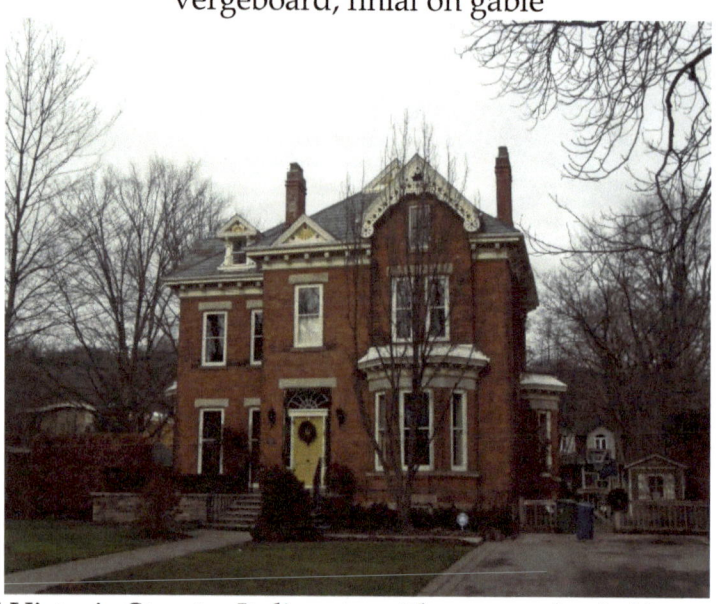

25 Victoria Street – Italianate with two-and-a-half storey tower-like bay, vergeboard trim, pediments on roof with decorative tympanum (also above dormer)

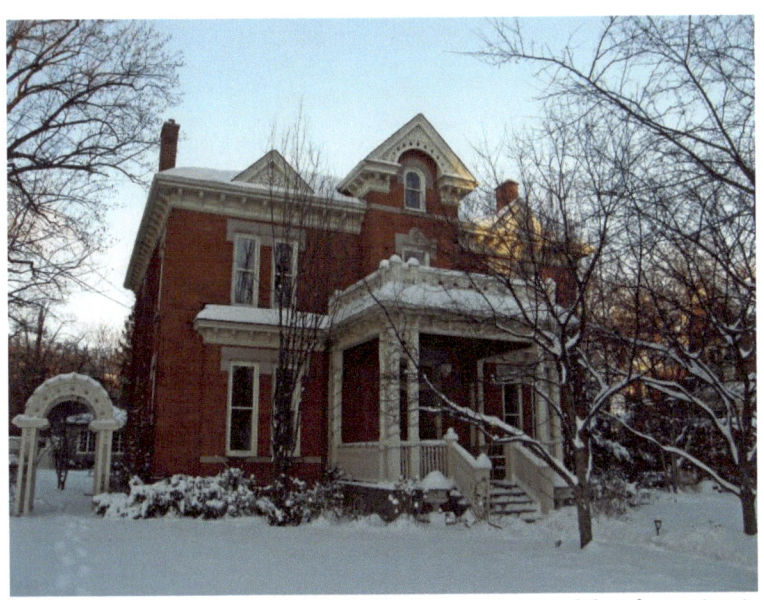

Italianate with two-and-a-half storey tower-like frontispiece,
vergeboard trim on gable, cornice brackets,
balcony above porch

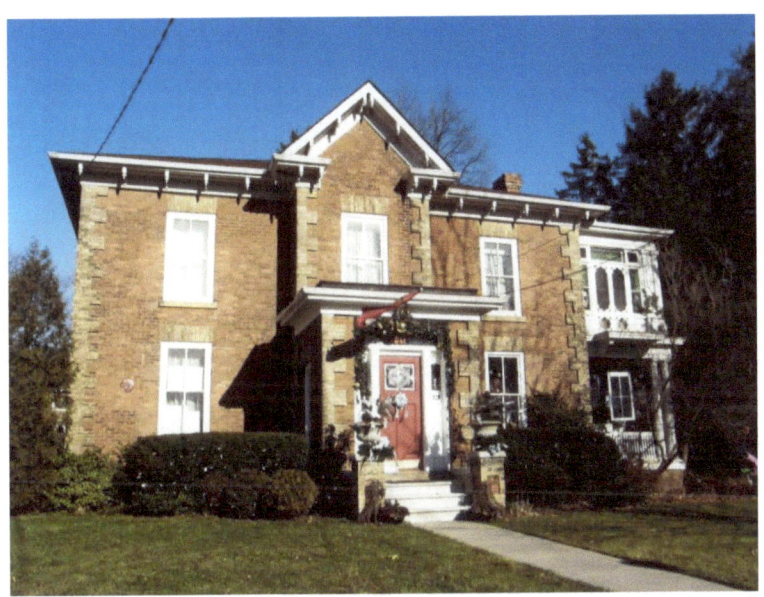

Italianate style with two-storey frontispiece, cornice brackets

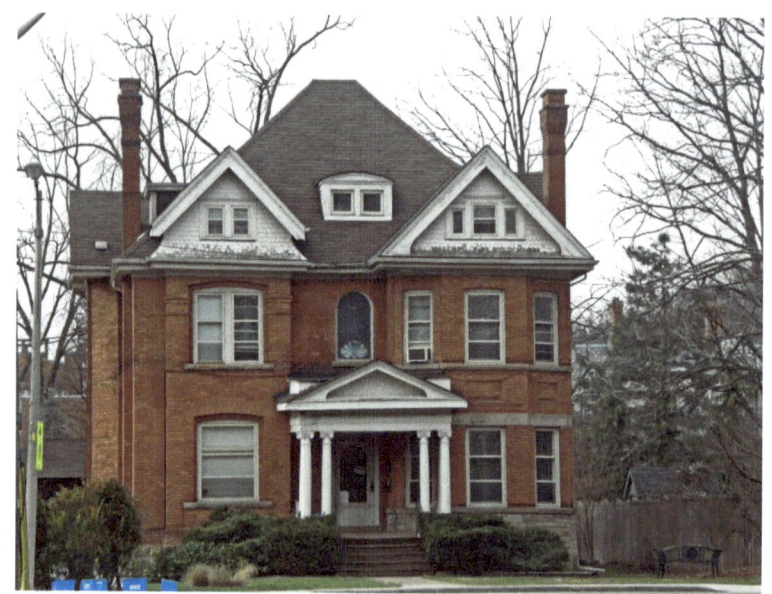

Dormers in attic, palladian window, verandah pillars with scroll-like capitals

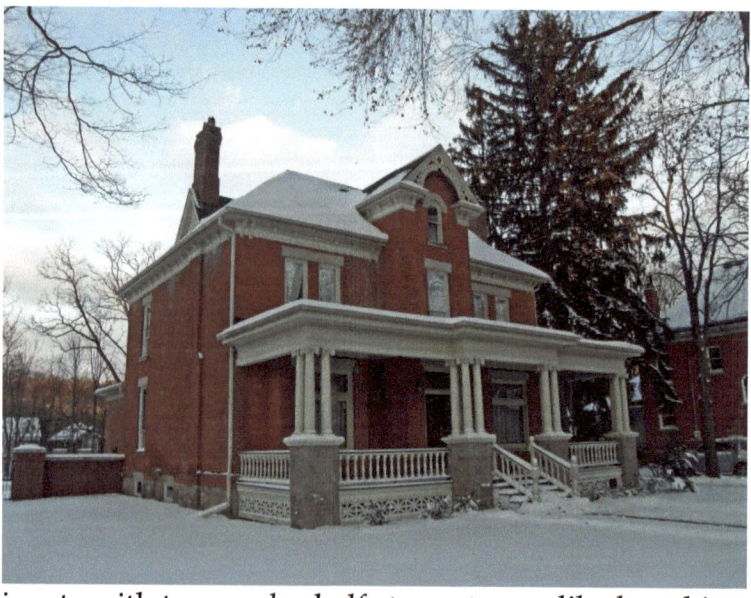

Italianate with two-and-a-half storey tower-like bay, hip roof

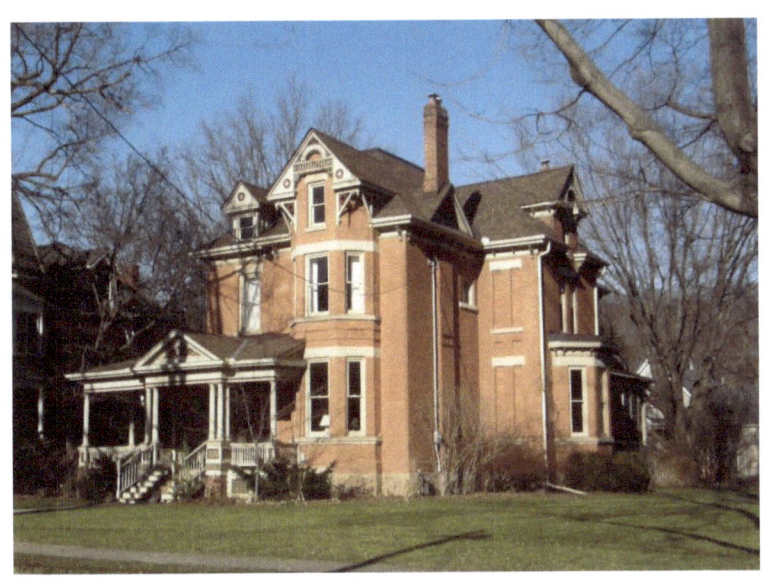

17 Victoria Street
Italianate with two-and-a-half storey tower-like bay on front
and side, decorated tympanum on pediment above verandah

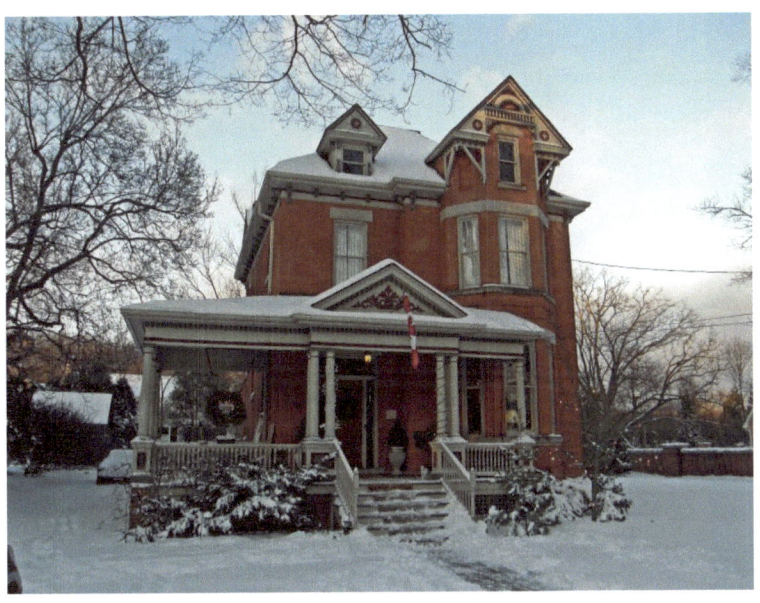

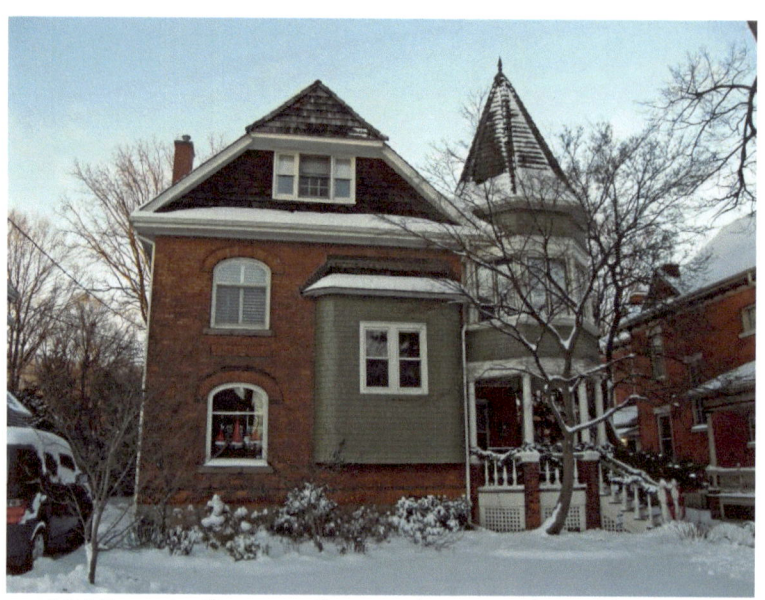

19 Victoria Street - Queen Anne style with turret

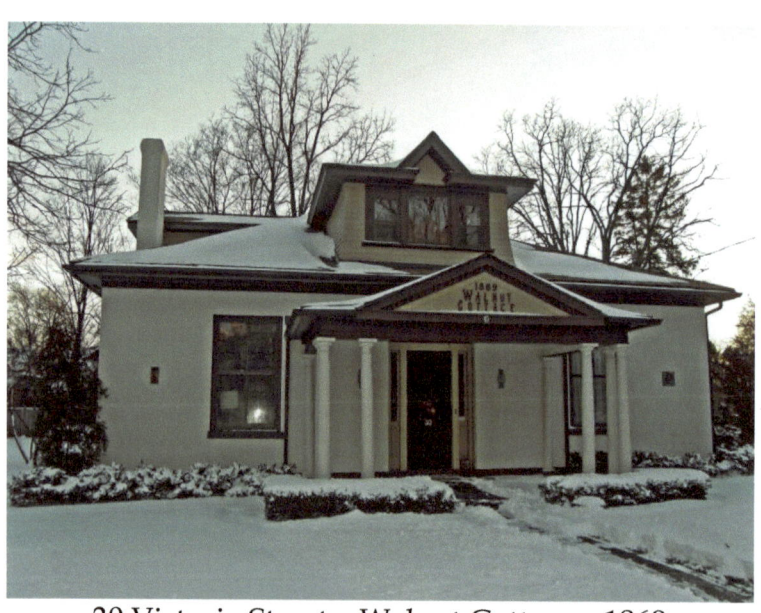

30 Victoria Street – Walnut Cottage - 1869

Grant Boulevard and area

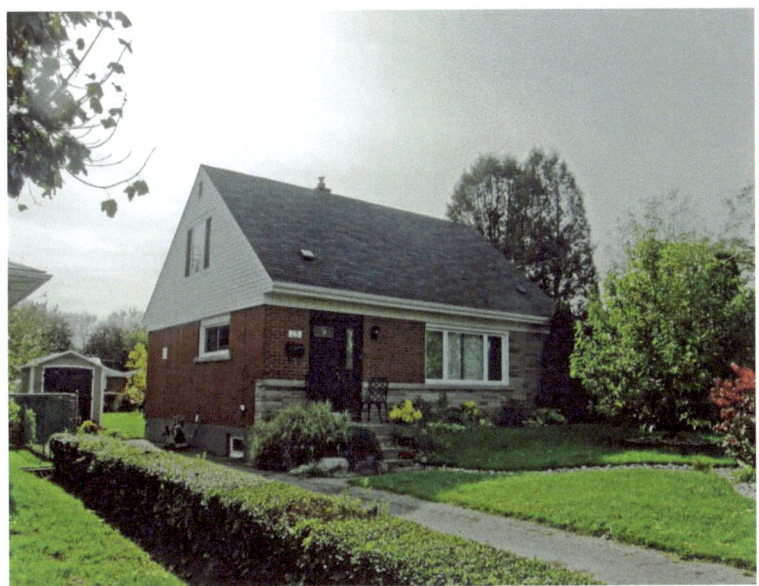

15 Grant Boulevard

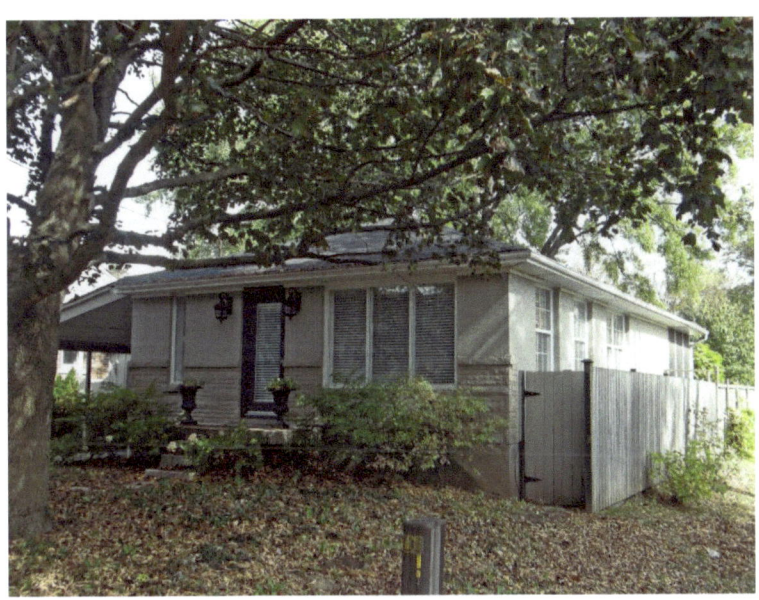

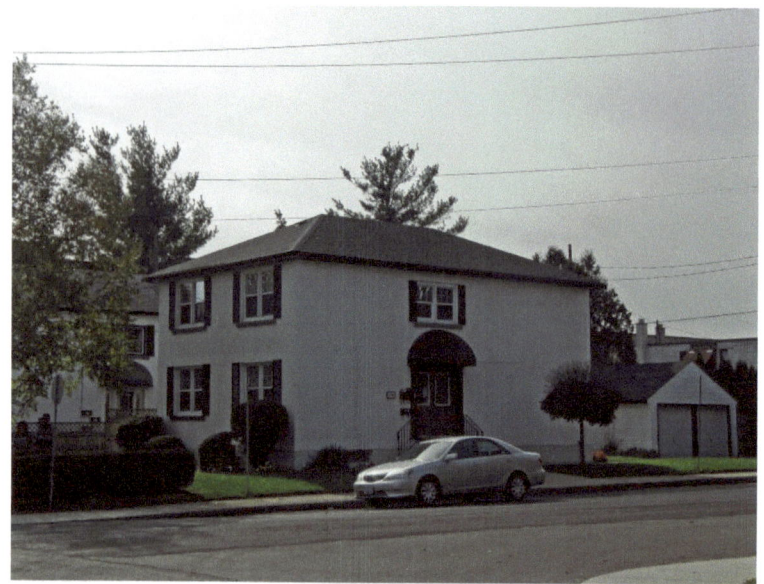

11 Don Street

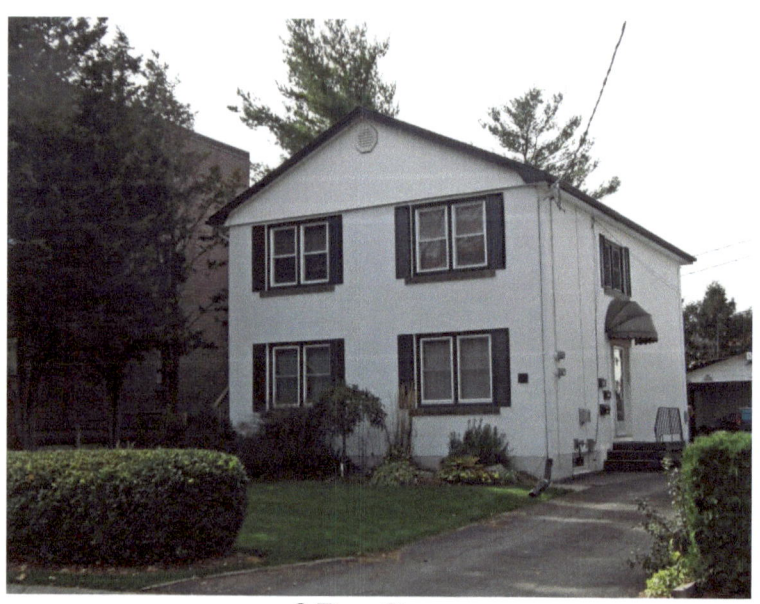

9 Don Street

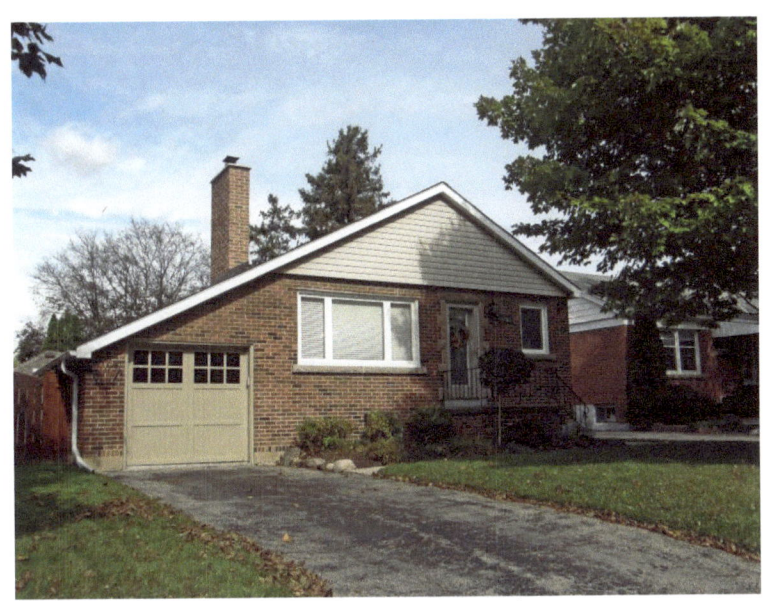

16 Grant Boulevard

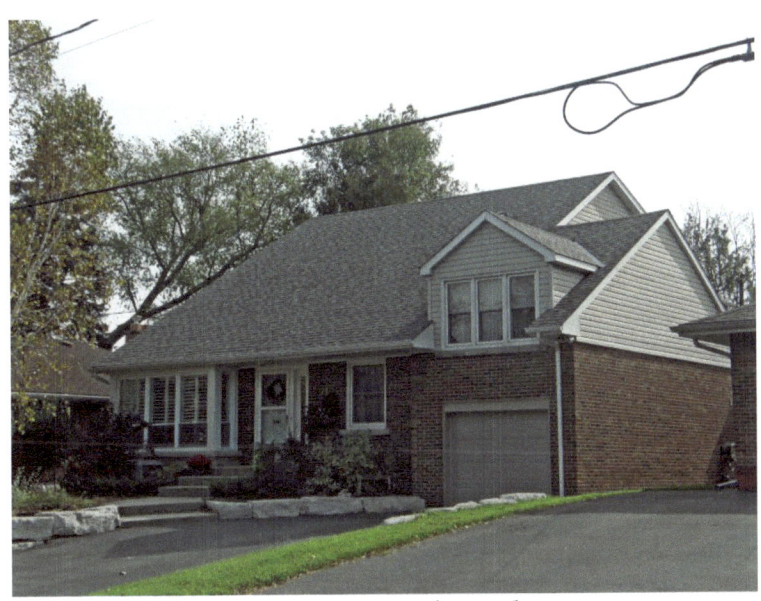

21 Grant Boulevard

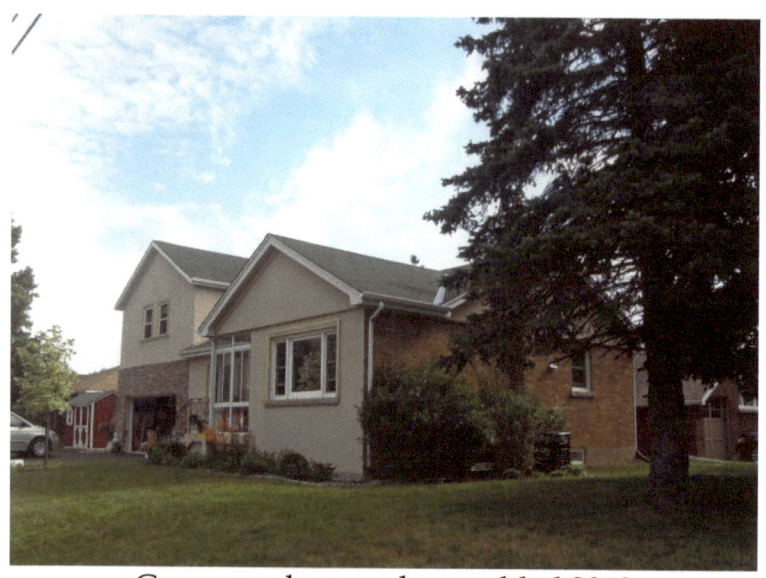

Garage and room above added 2010

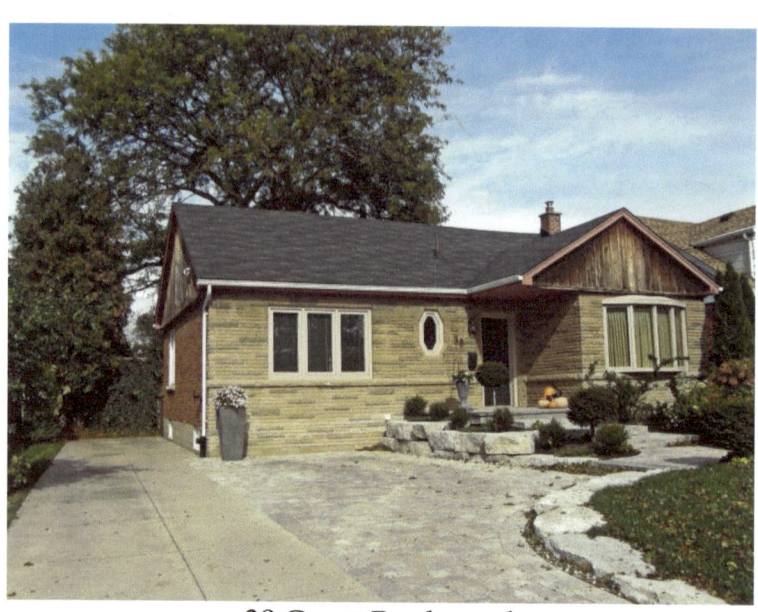

38 Grant Boulevard

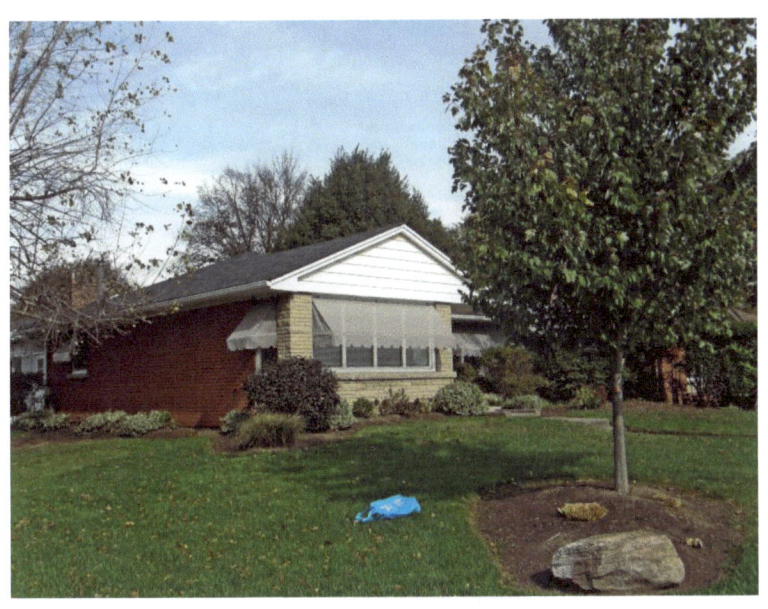

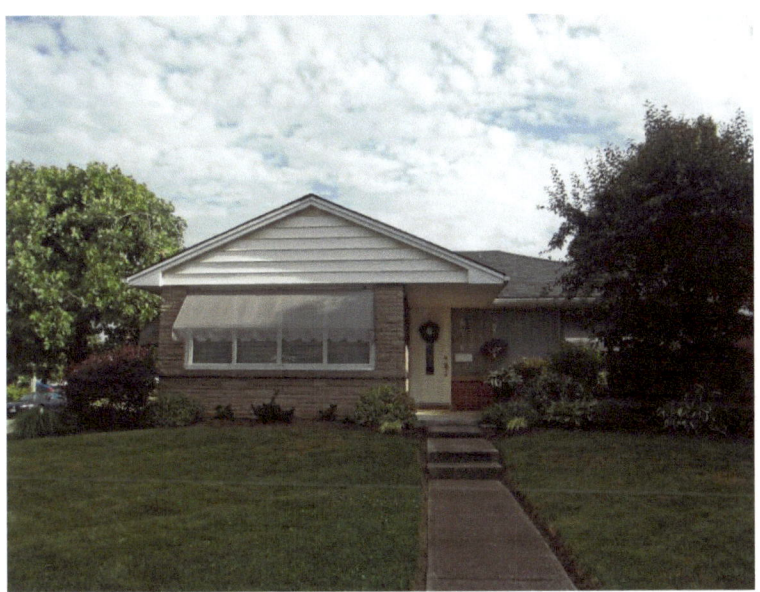

26 Grant Boulevard

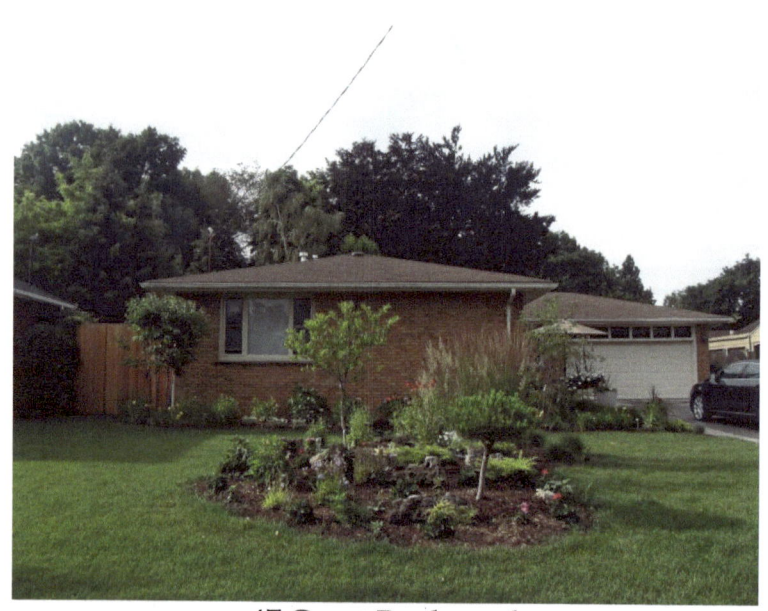

47 Grant Boulevard

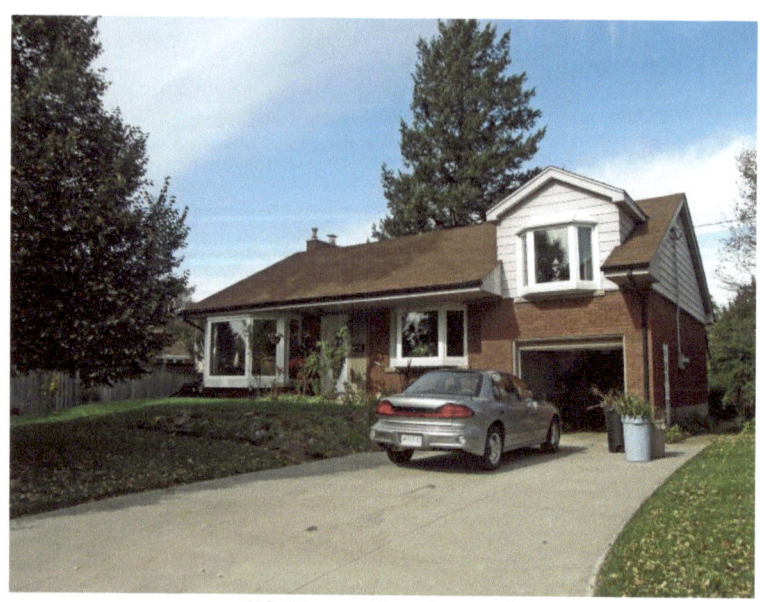

50 Grant Boulevard

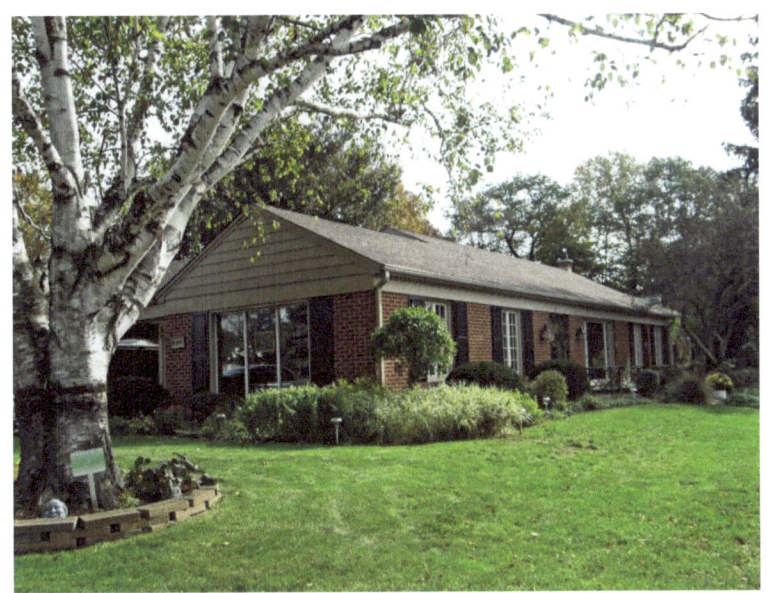

51 Grant Boulevard

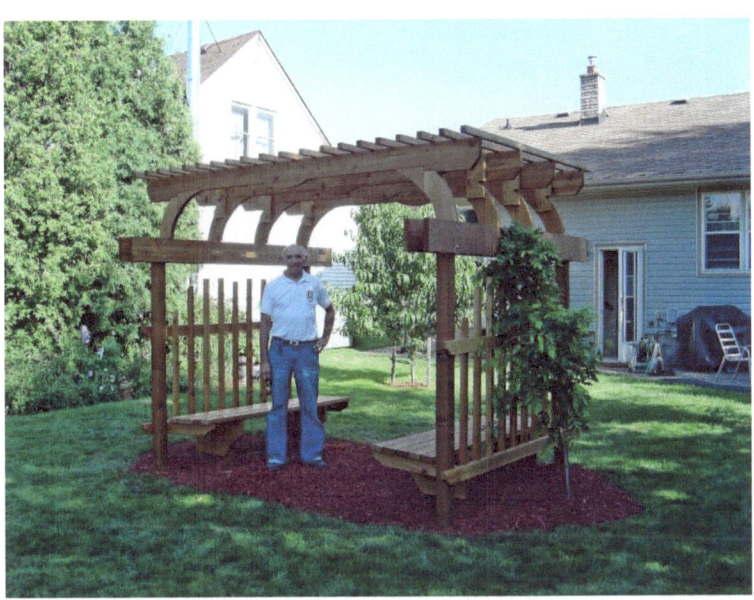

Arbour Harry built at 52 Grant Boulevard in 2005
Blue siding of house to the right of the picture

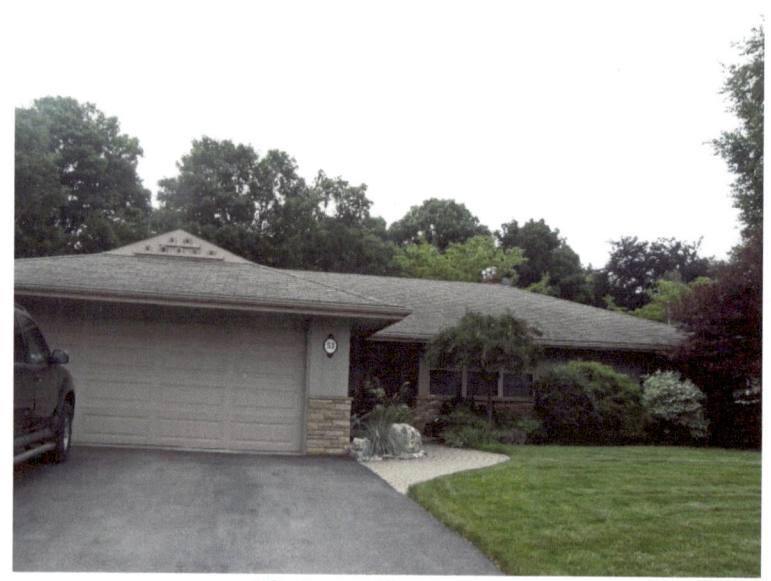

53 Grant Boulevard

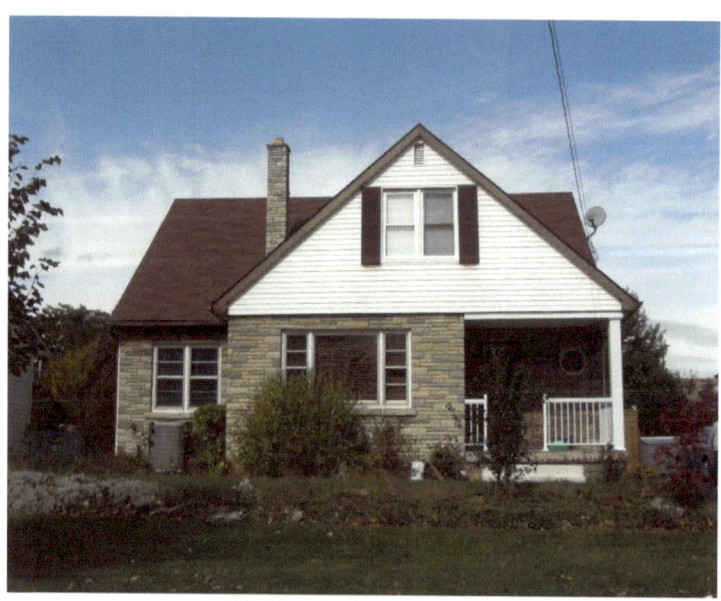

54 Grant Boulevard

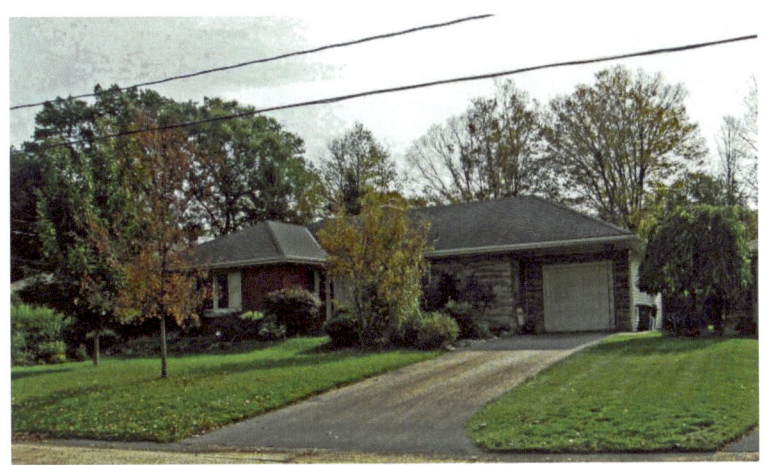

55 Grant Boulevard

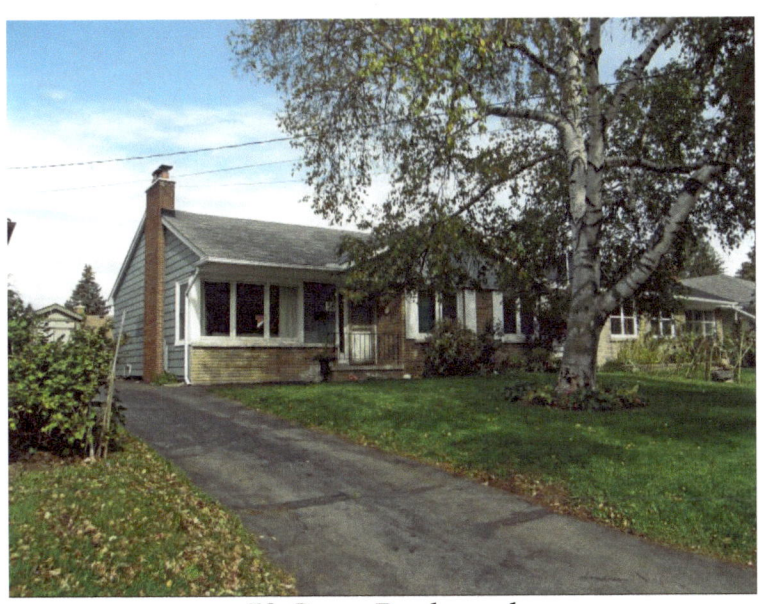

58 Grant Boulevard

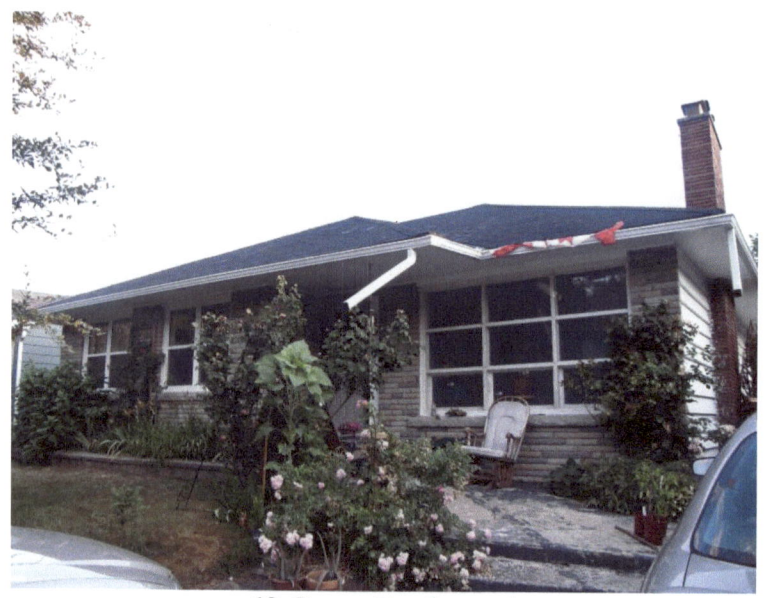

60 Grant Boulevard

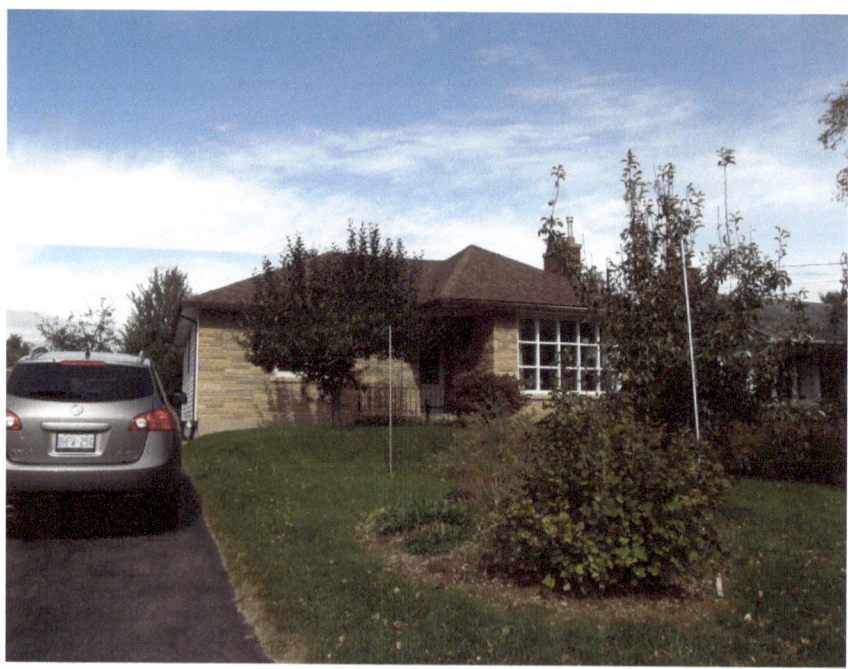

56 Grant Boulevard - Home of the Raues since August 2000
Built in 1953, one floor, three bedrooms, full basement

Brackets: a decorative or weight-bearing structural element which forms a right angle with one side against a wall and the other under a projecting surface such as an eave or roof. Example: Central Public School, Melville Street	
Capital: The uppermost finish or decoration on a column. Example: Victoria Street	
Cornice: originally the wooden overhang of the roof. With the use of stone, brick, iron and steel, the cornice is any projecting shelf at the top of a ceiling or roof. They can be very decorative. Example: 144 Melville Street	
Cornice Return: decorative element on the end of a gable. Example: 182 Melville Street	
Dentil Moulding: an even series of rectangles used as ornamental decoration in cornices.	
Dormer: (French for "sleep") a gable end window that pierces through the plane of a sloping roof surface to create usable space in the top floor or attic of a building by adding headroom. Example: 190 Melville Street	

Finial: ornament added to the top of a gable, pinnacle, canopy or spire – a Gothic element. Example: Victoria Street	
Fretwork: interlaced decorative design resembling a bracket Example: 141 Melville Street	
Gable: the triangular portion of a wall between the edges of a sloping roof. Example: 107 Melville Street	
Hipped Roof: a roof where all sides slope downwards to the walls with no gables. Example: 106 Melville Street	
Keystones and Voussoirs: a voussoir is a wedge-shaped element used in building an arch. A keystone is the central stone that locks all the stones into position, allowing the arch to bear weight. A keystone is often enlarged and embellished. Example: 141 Melville Street	
Quoin: masonry blocks at the corner of a wall, often a decorative feature, usually larger or of a different colour than the rest of the wall. Example: 124 Melville Street	

Palladian Window: a large window that is divided into three sections with the centre section larger than the two side sections and usually arched. Example: Victoria Street	
Pediment: a triangular section above the horizontal structure (entablature), typically supported by columns. The inside of the triangle is called the tympanum. Example: 113 Melville Street	
Turret: a small tower that projects from the wall of a building. Example: Victoria Street	
Vergeboards: also called bargeboards (gingerbread) – hang from the projecting end of a roof and are often elaborately carved and ornamented. Example: Victoria Street	

Dundas' Building Styles

Edwardian, 1900-1930 – This style bridges the ornate and elaborate styles of the Victorian era and the simplified styles of the 20th century. Balanced facades, simple roof lines, dormer windows, large front porches, and smooth brick surfaces are its characteristics. Example: 99 Melville Street	
Gothic Revival, 1830-1890 – These decorative buildings have sharply-pitched gables with highly detailed vergeboards, pointed-arch window openings, and dichromatic brickwork. It is a common style in Ontario. Example: Victoria Street	
Italianate, 1850-1900 – It has wide-bracketed eaves, belvederes, wrap-around verandahs. Example: 25 Victoria Street	

Queen Anne, 1885-1900 – This style is distinguished by an irregular outline featuring a combination of an offset tower, broad gables, projecting two-storey bays, verandahs, multi-sloped roofs, and tall, decorative chimneys. A mixture of brick and wood is common. Windows often have one large single-paned bottom sash and small panes in the upper sash. Example: 19 Victoria Street	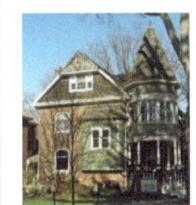
Regency Cottage, 1830-1860 – This style originated in England in 1815 and spread to Ontario later in the 19th century as British officers retired to Canada. It is a modest one-storey house with a low-pitched hip roof and has a symmetrical front façade. Example: 120 Melville Street	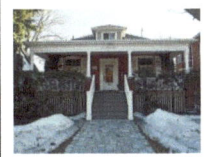